S. HRG. 113–463

INDISPENSABLE PARTNERS— REENERGIZING U.S.–INDIA TIES

HEARING

BEFORE THE

SUBCOMMITTEE ON NEAR EASTERN AND SOUTH AND CENTRAL ASIAN AFFAIRS

OF THE

COMMITTEE ON FOREIGN RELATIONS

UNITED STATES SENATE

ONE HUNDRED THIRTEENTH CONGRESS

SECOND SESSION

_____

JULY 16, 2014

_____

Printed for the use of the Committee on Foreign Relations

Available via the World Wide Web: http://www.gpo.gov/fdsys/

U.S. GOVERNMENT PRINTING OFFICE

91–143 PDF   WASHINGTON : 2014

CONTENTS

INDISPENSABLE PARTNERS—
REENERGIZING U.S.–INDIA TIES

WEDNESDAY, JULY 16, 2014

U.S. SENATE,
SUBCOMMITTEE ON NEAR EASTERN AND
SOUTH AND CENTRAL ASIA AFFAIRS,
COMMITTEE ON FOREIGN RELATIONS,
Washington, DC.

The subcommittee met, pursuant to notice, at 3:03 p.m., in room SD–419, Dirksen Senate Office Building, Hon. Tim Kaine (chairman of the subcommittee) presiding.

Present: Senators Kaine, Risch, and McCain.

OPENING STATEMENT OF HON. TIM KAINE,
U.S. SENATOR FROM VIRGINIA

Senator KAINE. If I could get everyone's attention, this meeting of the Senate Foreign Relations Committee Subcommittee on Near East, South, and Central Asian Affairs will come to order. This is a very great set of panels on a very important topic. Senator Risch is on his way. He should be here in just a couple of minutes, and we expect other colleagues may join us during the hearing. But I want to welcome all to this hearing today.

The title of the hearing is "Indispensable Partners—Reenergizing U.S.-India Ties." I generally am not a fan of the word "indispensable." There is a great quote attributed to De Gaulle: "The graveyards are filled with indispensable men." No matter how much we think things are indispensable or people are indispensable, the answer is we are usually wrong. But in this case we advisedly chose to use that word because we do think the partnership between the United States and India meets the high standard of what "indispensable" means.

This is an important and propitious time with a new Government in India and a forthcoming visit of the Indian Prime Minister, Prime Minister Modi, here to the United States in the fall. So we are very, very glad to have two good panels with witnesses both from the United States Government and longtime United States-India experts who are here to illuminate us about opportunities and challenges and the path forward.

I had the wonderful fortune of serving as Governor of Virginia and working very closely with both the Virginia Indian-American community, but also with significant trade opportunities with Indian businesses. One of the first business deals I did as Governor—I will always remember this—in a part of the State that had been hit very, very hard by NAFTA, that had lost a lot of jobs after the NAFTA Treaty was signed, Danville, VA, on the North Carolina border, an economic development deal was done in a closed manufacturing plant, where Indian venture capitalists purchased an English plastic polymer company, decided that they needed to have a U.S. manufacturing facility, purchased the closed plant in Danville and hired a Spaniard to be the plant operator.

When I went to the plant opening in Danville, VA, and I saw not only a United States and Virginia flag, but an Indian flag, a United Kingdom flag, and a Spanish flag, I knew something about the importance of this partnership. And it has worked out very, very well.

But we are here at an important time. The United States-India relationship has grown tremendously in the 6 years since the signing of the landmark United States-India civil nuclear deal. Some examples of activity in the last 6 years: The United States and India participate in more than three dozen dialogues covering a wide array of cooperative activities: clean energy, peacekeeping, counterterrorism, health.

Bilateral trade in goods and services between our nations has reached nearly $100 billion. In 2013 India was the single largest country market for the Export-Import Bank, with authorizations of $2.1 billion. The Partnership to Advance Clean Energy has mobilized $2 billion in public and private resources for clean energy projects in India. Our defense trade, which has kind of been a recent arrival on the scene in terms of cooperation, has taken off and been very successful, nearly $10 billion, with billions more in the pipeline.

Over 100,000 Indian students are currently studying in U.S. universities. According to the latest Pew Global Attitude Survey, released just this week, over 55 percent of Indians hold a very positive view of the United States.

When asked what country would most likely be India's leading ally, the United States came in at numer one.

It is not just about polls and it is not just about trade. It is also about common democratic values. Maybe that is the primary thing, the world's oldest democracy and the world's largest democracy, and the people-to-people ties and the business linkages we have are very important.

The 3-million-strong Indian Americans who contribute across this country to the professions and to the entrepreneurship and the civic life and academia and every other walk of life serve as and important bridge between our two countries. Global connections is a key to economic success today and a person is a global connection if that person has ties, as so many of our Indian-American citizens do.

I was reminded of this last week at a dinner I attended hosted by the Indian Ambassador to the United States. CEO's of major American companies, Pepsi and MasterCard, were in attendance. Both hale from the Indian-American community. Just in Virginia, more than 100,000 Indian-Americans call Virginia home, and we have some spectacular, successful businesses.

One example in Virginia I am proud of, Husk Power. It is an innovative company. It was founded by graduates of the University of Virginia. I know that Nisha Biswal will approve of that as a Cavalier herself. The innovative company provides electricity to over 200,000 rural Indian households using biomass. So Indian American professionals from an American university, UVA, doing a wonderful project that is providing significant benefit in India.

Now, any relationship between partners is bound to have some friction, and there has been friction in the last 6 years. That is necessary. You do not ever test a friendship until you have disagreements, and so disagreements occur and the test of the friendship is whether we can work through them.

But the strategic rationale behind the partnership is only growing more important every day. There is increasing instability around the globe in Syria and Iraq, Russia and Ukraine, China in the South China Sea. Both India and the United States notice that, care about it, want to be productive in helping solve it. So cultivating this partnership in 2014 with the new government in India is critically important.

The relationship is important today and it will grow.

India is bound to become the world's most populous nation and the third-leading economy by 2030. It is a democracy where the median age is 25. Fifty years from now the relationship will directly affect the strategic and economic interests of the entire United States and impact ordinary Americans, as it does today.

So we need the United States and India to be joint stakeholders, to uphold global norms and rules of the road.

India will need our partnership as it shoulders global responsibilities and expands its economy to meet its own developmental goals. So that is why we need to get the relationship right and that is why the committee is holding the hearing today. The engagement has to be driven by a sense of realism and realistic assumptions and shared interests. It has to avoid just being transactional and keep in mind both long-term strategic goals, but also a sense of the shared values that animate both nations.

So I look forward to hearing today how the United States intends to capitalize on the new phase in the United States-India relationship, particularly in the areas of strategic and regional cooperation, defense ties, and our business and economic engagement.

I would like to now ask my ranking member on the subcommittee, Senator Risch, for opening comments. Following that I will introduce panel one and we will get right to the testimony and questions.

OPENING STATEMENT OF HON. JAMES E. RISCH, U.S. SENATOR FROM IDAHO

Senator RISCH. Well, thank you very much, Chairman Kaine.

It has been a while since this committee has taken the time to evaluate the United States-India relationship and it is appropriate that we do so at this time, particularly in light of the changes that we see going forward. Fortunately, changes in India present new opportunities to move our bilateral relationship forward.

Specifically, I am encouraged by Prime Minister Modi's victory and I know there is a lot of hope that Modi wants to revive India's economic growth, rein in corruption, encourage the private sector, and create jobs. This will require tough decisions to be made, but the election provides him with a mandate to make them.

Economic reforms will be incredibly important to create a fair and equal playing field to lure more foreign investment. This is why I hope we can conclude a bilateral investment treaty quickly, increase United States direct investment in India, and, very importantly, improve intellectual property protections. Those type of protections are absolutely necessary for any economy hoping to move forward.

One area of particular interest to me is civilian nuclear cooperation. Much of the technical cooperation between the United States and India on nuclear power is led by the great people at the Idaho National Laboratory located in eastern Idaho. Just last week, the laboratory hosted the latest meeting of the U.S.-India Civil Nuclear Energy Working Group. This is a great partnership.

However, we need to move beyond the technical cooperation and research. It has been 6 years since the United States-India nuclear deal was completed and we have yet to see United States nuclear companies have the ability to participate in India. I hope we can see improvement on the liability issues and I urge the parties to move quickly to resolve those issues. This will result in the relationship deepening and it will be a great benefit to both parties.

Defense cooperation and security are also important arenas where we can and should increase our collaboration. India is a pivotal country and can be a crucial partner to maintaining stability in the Indo-Pacific region. The United States can help India modernize its military, especially in light of other powers that are advancing in the region.

There is already good cooperation through the U.S.-India Defense, Trade, and Technology Initiative, but there is room for deeper engagement. India's willingness to adhere to and increase United States technology protection agreements will be critical to moving the United States-India defense partnership forward.

Again, Mr. Chairman, I think it is very appropriate to hold this hearing at this time. Thank you for doing so.

Senator KAINE. Thank you, Senator Risch.

Now on to the witnesses. We are glad to be joined by Senator McCain, who recently returned from a trip to India, and glad that he is with us as well. Our first panel has two witnesses. Nisha Biswal was sworn in as the Assistant Secretary of State for South and Central Asian Affairs in October 2013. She has been before the Foreign Relations Committee a number of times recently. Previously she served as the Assistant Administrator for Asia at USAID. She holds a bachelor's degree from the University of Virginia.

Dr. Amy Searight is Deputy Assistant Secretary of Defense for South and Southeast Asia. She is a principal adviser to senior leadership within the DOD for all policy matters that pertain to the development and implementation of joint defense strategies within this region. Dr. Searight, it is great to have you as well.

I would like to begin with Secretary Biswal, if you would give your opening testimony, followed by Dr. Searight, and then we will move to questions.

STATEMENT OF HON. NISHA D. BISWAL, ASSISTANT SECRETARY FOR SOUTH AND CENTRAL ASIAN AFFAIRS, U.S. DEPARTMENT OF STATE, WASHINGTON, DC

Ms. BISWAL. Chairman Kaine, Ranking Member Risch, thank you very much for inviting me to testify today and for holding this very timely hearing. I am pleased to be here with Dr. Searight, a close friend and colleague. In the interest of time, I will summarize my statement and ask that the full testimony be submitted for the record.

Senator, this is indeed an important time to reexamine the United States-India relationship. The historic elections this spring conferred an unprecedented mandate on Prime Minister Modi to create a historic opportunity as well in reenergizing our relationship with India. I was in New Delhi last week with Deputy Secretary Bill Burns to meet with Prime Minister Modi and key members of his Cabinet. Our trip was on the heels of the visit by Senator McCain, who was there previously, the previous week, and again demonstrated that as far as the United States-India relationship is concerned that this is deeply a bipartisan supported relationship in the United States.

In fact, we noted during our meetings that successive administrations, Democratic and Republican, have made the strategic bet that a rising India is fundamentally in the United States interest. Asian economies will play a greater role in shaping the global economic landscape in the years to come and will also be of greater consequence on ensuring regional security. A strong and prosperous India, with its democratic values, as you noted, Mr. Chairman, and its entrepreneurial spirit, will play a critical role in shaping that landscape and will be an increasingly important partner for the United States in the Asia-Pacific region.

But if India is to achieve its economic and strategic potential, it will need to address the myriad economic and governance challenges that it faces. Much of the excitement that has been generated by the new Modi government in India and around the world, and most notably in the business community, has been around this idea of accountable and effective government that can unleash India's economic potential.

As we are invested in the strategic importance of a rising India, we are also economically invested in India's growth. We think our economies, our businesses, our universities, and our peoples can partner and collaborate in helping India realize its vision and its potential. Our two countries are already more heavily invested in each other's prosperity than ever before. Our trade has grown fivefold since 2000, to almost $100 billion annually, and we are focused on growing that fivefold again to half a trillion, as Vice President Biden has challenged us.

American companies recognize the tremendous potential of India's economy and are eager to make long-term investments in India. As trade has grown, inevitably we have also had some areas of disagreement and some areas of friction, as you noted. We are committed to addressing those areas of friction through dialogue and engagement, and we are optimistic that this new government will take the necessary steps to promote long-term growth.

Areas of cooperation include energy as one of the brightest areas, where India is meeting—we are helping India meet its growing energy needs, as well as creating opportunities for our own businesses, through contracts on the export of American liquefied natural gas, identifying unconventional energy resources, clean energy resources, and fulfilling the promise of delivering cutting edge United States nuclear energy technologies, as Senator Risch mentioned, collaborating on other areas of energy security.

While my colleague Dr. Searight will discuss in more detail the defense partnership, I simply want to underscore the centrality of our security engagement with India to the United States-India partnership. We are committed to a strong and capable India that will advance stability and security across the Indo-Pacific.

The locus of our convergent strategic interests is in Asia and, as Prime Minister Modi demonstrated with his invitation to regional leaders at his inauguration, India has set out that it will be a more consequential and influential relationship in the region. We welcome that initiative because strong Indian leadership is very much in our interest, whether in supporting a successful security and political transition in Afghanistan, bolstering trade and economic connectivity between South and Southeast Asia, improving relations between India and Pakistan, combating the threats of terrorism and violent extremism.

Our bilateral engagements over the course of the next several months will reinforce our strategic, security, economic, and people-to-people ties. As Secretary Kerry is planning to travel to New Delhi later this month to cochair the next round of the U.S.-India Strategic Dialogue, we see new possibilities for advancing that partnership. The strategic dialogue will kick off a series of high-level engagements throughout the late summer and into the fall, culminating in the visit of Prime Minister Modi to Washington at the invitation of President Obama.

But, Mr. Chairman, the true potential of this relationship was probably best captured by Prime Minister Modi when he said to us last week that this is a relationship not just about the benefits it brings to the Indian people or the American people, but that its true value is that when the world's largest democracy and the world's oldest democracy come together the world stands to benefit.

We deeply appreciate that framing and we deeply appreciate the engagement and support that this relationship enjoys across the United States. The U.S. Congress and this body has played an important role in continuing to advance the partnership and we look forward to working with you as we move forward in the months ahead.

With that, Mr. Chairman, I look forward to answering any questions that you may have.

[The prepared statement of Ms. Biswal follows:]

PREPARED STATEMENT OF NISHA D. BISWAL

Chairman Kaine, Ranking Member Risch, thank you for inviting me to testify before you today. It is an honor to appear before this committee, and I'm pleased to speak alongside my colleague, Deputy Assistant Secretary of Defense for South and Southeast Asia, Amy Searight.

This is indeed an important time to reexamine U.S.-India relations. The historic elections this spring, which brought a record 530 million voters to the polls and conferred an unprecedented mandate on Prime Minister Narendra Modi and the Bharatiya Janata Party, also created a historic opportunity to reenergize our relationship.

Mr. Chairman, successive administrations have made the strategic bet that a rising India is in the U.S. interest. Our rebalance to the Asia-Pacific is premised on the consequential role the region's 4.3 billion people will play in global politics, security, and economics in the 21st century. The continent's success will depend on choices Asian nations and their partners make. A strong India will play a critical role in the coming decades in shaping this Asian landscape, and our partnership with India will play an increasingly important role in that context.

But if India is to achieve its economic and strategic potential, it must grapple with the myriad economic and governance challenges it is facing, including slow growth, energy shortages, and flagging foreign investment.

I had the opportunity to accompany Deputy Secretary Bill Burns to India last week to meet with Prime Minister Modi and key members of his cabinet to discuss their economic and security agenda, as well as the U.S.-India relationship. The Modi government has identified infrastructure, manufacturing, modernizing the military, energy security, attracting greater foreign investment, and expanding access to skills training and education as its key priorities. The Prime Minister, in inviting regional leaders to his inauguration, also signaled that India will play a greater strategic role in its immediate neighborhood and across the Indo-Pacific region. For India to achieve its potential, Prime Minister Modi has said that one of his top priorities will be efficient, effective, and accountable governance.

In all the areas that the Modi government has identified as priorities, we think the United States, including our businesses and universities, can play an important role in helping address the challenges India faces and creating opportunities that benefit both countries. But the true potential of the relationship is best captured in what Prime Minister Modi said to Deputy Secretary Burns last week. He noted that he does not see our relations in terms of the benefits it brings to the Indian people or the American people—that goes without saying. The true power and potential of this relationship, he said, is that when the world's oldest democracy and the world's largest democracy come together, the world will benefit.

Mr. Chairman, we are confident we can work in a strong and collaborative partnership with the Modi government to grow our economic and strategic relations with India in a way that benefits both countries and both economies. But we also believe the true measure of this partnership, which President Obama said will be one of the defining partnerships of the 21st century, is its potential to address global challenges and, as the Prime Minister noted, to benefit the world.

ECONOMIC AND TRADE PARTNERSHIP

Our two countries have never been more invested in each other's economic future. India's goal of building a strong and integrated economy that is led by private-sector growth and boasts a global reach, will offer sustainable, long-term market opportunities for U.S. firms.

With annual two-way trade in goods and services of almost $100 billion in 2013— up 61 percent from 2009 and over 400 percent since 2000—we already enjoy an important commercial relationship with India. We're focused on growing that fivefold again, a goal Vice President Biden set last year on his visit to India. To achieve that ambitious figure, American companies need to believe that the benefits of trade with India outweigh the costs and the challenges—and that India remains committed to growth over the long term.

One way to strengthen two-way investment and ensure increased opportunities for U.S. businesses in India is through a Bilateral Investment Treaty (BIT). A BIT with India would help support key economic objectives for both countries, from protection of investment interests overseas to the promotion of market-oriented policies and exports.

A BIT would also greatly improve two-way investment flows. That's good for the U.S. economy. Increasing Indian foreign direct investment in the United States would expand U.S. jobs in a variety of professional, scientific, and technical sectors that have traditionally attracted Indian investment. Trade expansion also benefits families and businesses by supporting productive, high-paying jobs in exports and increasing the variety of products available for purchase.

American companies recognize the tremendous potential of India's economy and are eager to make long-term investments in India. U.S. companies—boasting the highest standards and highest quality products and services—can play an invaluable role in transforming the Indian economy through partnerships for joint innovation and development. Cross-pollination of U.S. and Indian businesses is a win-win for our economies and will create thousands of jobs in both our countries.

Higher education is a vital part of our economic agenda. Indian students comprise the second-largest group of foreign students in the United States, with 100,000 students studying in the United States in 2012–13. Not only do they contribute over $3 billion to the U.S. economy every year, they also advance innovation and research in our universities.

Our education partnership is not focused only on universities. Mr. Chairman, in your home State of Virginia and throughout the United States, community colleges are working with Indian counterparts to strengthen the connection between industry and education. Working with the Indian Government, we are keen to help India adapt our community-college model to meet its skills needs and goal of building 10,000 community colleges by 2030, so that India's future workforce can benefit from one of our Nation's greatest exports, knowledge, and skill development.

As trade has grown by a factor of five in 15 years, inevitably we have also had some disagreements over trade. We're committed to addressing trade frictions through dialogue and engagement. We appreciate the huge strides India has made over the past two decades, benefiting from trade liberalization and reappraising decades-old orthodoxies. While India is still ranked 134 out of 189 countries in the World Bank's Ease of Doing Business ranking, the new government is already taking decisive steps to make India more open to the foreign businesses and investment that can help stimulate greater growth.

On July 10, the Indian Government unveiled its Union Budget for consideration by Parliament. There is much for us to take note of, including efforts by the government to stimulate growth; curb borrowing; and reduce barriers to investment in defense, insurance, e-commerce, transportation infrastructure, and real estate. We are studying the budget proposal closely, and we will continue to follow the parliamentary debates as the budget bill moves forward. In fact, a senior delegation led by Assistant Secretary of Commerce Arun Kumar, along with officials from USTR and the State Department, is in India right now, engaging with the new government on a broad range of economic issues.

To fully realize its economic potential, India also needs to foster inclusive and sustainable growth. While women continue to rise to the highest positions in civil society, business, and government, in many ways the potential of women and girls in India remains untapped and underutilized as a force for growth and development. Fundamental issues of women's security and opportunity need to be addressed, so that Indian women can achieve their full potential and make their contribution to India's growth story. As President Obama has said, "When women succeed, nations are more safe, more secure, and more prosperous." We know that securing equal rights and opportunity for women and girls is not only the right thing to do, but the smart thing to do.

Climate change is another issue that all emerging economies, including India, are grappling with. For growth to be enduring, it must be environmentally sustainable. We enjoy a broad range of bilateral cooperation with India on clean energy and climate issues, including Secretary Kerry's Climate Change Working Group. Our cooperation on mitigating the causes and effects of climate change, including investment and development of clean and renewable energy sources, is increasingly a whole-of-government effort. It is our hope this bilateral cooperation can lead to greater collaboration in multilateral fora.

ENERGY AND INNOVATION

We have seen tremendous progress in our energy cooperation since the launch of the U.S.-India Energy Dialogue in 2005. This forum has brought our governments and private sectors together to expand cooperation on nuclear energy, electrical grid and power generation, energy efficiency, and oil and gas exploration. It has also expanded markets for renewable energy technologies and lowered barriers to clean energy deployment. The Energy Dialogue—along with the Energy Security Roundtable—has leveraged each country's strengths in research, opened opportunities for American businesses and technologies, and strengthened India's energy security and economic growth.

Under the Partnership to Advance Clean Energy, we have mobilized over $2 billion of public and private investment in solar, biofuels, building efficiency, and other areas. Our energy relationship is also expanding through contracts for the export of American liquefied natural gas, by together identifying unconventional energy resources, and by fulfilling the promise of delivering cutting-edge U.S. nuclear energy technology to meet Indian energy needs. These are top priorities for the United States and India.

One fast-growing area of partnership is our robust science and technology cooperation. Our collaboration sustains economic growth and job creation, while helping our citizens to live longer, healthier lives. We will showcase this partnership later this year in New Delhi at the U.S.-India Technology Summit, which will enable new partnerships in innovation and technology development, stemming from breakthroughs our scientists and engineers have already achieved together.

The intersection of innovation and health will provide the next frontier of partnership for the United States and India, with global implications. Already, our two countries are deploying a rotavirus vaccine, ROTAVAC, the product of a public-private partnership that has the potential to save hundreds of thousands of young lives in India as well as around the world.

We are also expanding our efforts in space exploration and science. NASA has collaborated with the Indian Space Research Organization to share navigation expertise for India's Mars Orbiter Mission, and we are exploring even more opportunities for collaboration through our Civil Space Joint Working Group.

SECURITY

While my colleague will discuss the future of defense trade and cooperation, I would like to underline the centrality of our security engagement to the U.S.-India partnership. We are committed to a strong and influential India in the security realm.

Take, for instance, the impressive growth in our counterterrorism (CT) and security cooperation over the last several years. This includes the December 2013 conference in New Delhi on mega-city policing, which focused on domestic terrorism, emergency disaster response, corruption, and other challenges faced by major cities in both countries.

India remains an active and strong CT partner of the United States. Our cooperation has already brought to justice several Mumbai terrorists, including David Headley and Ajmal Kasab. Five years after the terrorist assault on Mumbai, the United States stands with the people of India in mourning the loss of innocent lives, including six Americans, and seeking justice. As President Obama has stated, the Mumbai perpetrators, financers, and sponsors must be held accountable for their crimes, and we have called on all governments to do just that. We will also continue to work together to track and disrupt terrorism, including those responsible for the Indian consulate attack in Herat.

REGIONAL COOPERATION

As I noted at the outset, the locus of our convergent strategic interests is in Asia. We are confident that a strong U.S.-India partnership will help us address shared challenges and seize shared opportunities.

When Prime Minister Modi invited the Prime Minister of Pakistan, Nawaz Sharif, and the leaders of South Asia Association for Regional Cooperation (SAARC) countries to his inauguration ceremony, he demonstrated his firm commitment to strengthening India's ties with its immediate region. That's good news for India and the region, and greatly beneficial to global stability.

In South Asia, where intraregional commerce comprises only 5 percent of total trade, and intraregional investment a paltry 1 percent of investment flows, India has a chance to bring its entire neighborhood along with it, enhancing prosperity and peace by boosting trade and building connectivity throughout South Asia and the Bay of Bengal region. That India trades much more with Europe, the United States, and the Middle East than with its immediate South Asian neighbors is a global economic anomaly, one that India can help address by shaping a connectivity network between India, South Asia, and the rest of the continent. The United States welcomes the new government's efforts to strengthen SAARC, and we were pleased to see Indian Minister of External Affairs Sushma Swaraj make her first official visit abroad to Bangladesh in late June.

We are also confident that the United States can play a helpful role in facilitating trade and connectivity in South Asia, through our New Silk Road and Indo-Pacific Economic Corridor strategies. American firms have voiced strong support for our leadership in the region, noting that U.S. technology should be instrumental in developing cross-border ties in the region.

Where do our comparative advantages lie? The United States has a tremendous opportunity to encourage physical connectivity by expanding port and ''last mile'' connectivity across the Bay of Bengal region, and linking key Indian, Bangladeshi, and Burmese transit hubs; to help shape regional regulatory architecture through regional trade and transit agreements, improving the investment climate for greater foreign direct investment, and reducing nontariff trade barriers throughout South

Asia; and to foster human connectivity by linking government officials, business leaders, think tanks, and civil society.

We support increasing trade and investment between India and Pakistan, and reducing trade barriers. Increased economic cooperation will improve the long-term prosperity of both nations and the entire region. Trade between India and Pakistan in 2013 was a relatively meager $2.5 billion. There's no reason that figure can't quadruple to $10 billion, with steps to ease trade barriers and open up new market and investment opportunities.

Further west, India shares our goal of a successful transformation in Afghanistan. We both want to ensure the peace and stability of a democratic Afghanistan, and help it economically integrate further into the South and Central Asia region. Our bilateral and trilateral discussions on Afghanistan help advance our economic, political, and security objectives.

Both our nations watch developments in the Middle East with a close eye. We share concerns about the situation in Iraq. India has been supportive of the P5+1 process and a partner in our efforts to limit Iranian oil exports as we seek a negotiated solution to the Iranian nuclear issue. And our efforts to address trafficking in persons and labor concerns in the gulf benefit millions of expatriate Indian workers there.

We have expanded our regional consultations with India to include South, Central, West, and East Asia. We will hold new rounds of several of these dialogues in the months to come, and are exploring how to elevate these discussions further. These consultations are not just a talk shop: The U.S.-India-Japan trilateral dialogue has deepened our partnership on our Indo-Pacific Economic Corridor agenda, maritime security, humanitarian assistance and disaster planning, as well as coordination in multilateral fora. Last year, with the support of India, we participated in the Indian Ocean Regional Association as a dialogue partner for the first time.

While some believe our renewed strategic commitment to India comes at the expense of other regional powers, we see it differently. We welcome the rise of any power in Asia that upholds global norms and contributes to the stability and prosperity of the continent. We also welcome, with India, the opportunity to showcase the commonalities that bind the largest democracies in the Indo-Pacific region, including India, Indonesia, Australia, Japan, and the United States.

LOOKING AHEAD

With a solid foundation to work from, our bilateral engagements over the course of the next several months will reinforce our strategic, economic, and people-to-people ties. Already, India's newly appointed Minister for Health and Family Welfare, Dr. Harsh Vardhan, visited Washington and several other cities in the United States to explore how to enhance our U.S.-India Health Initiative, and make more progress together in improving child health in India. I was particularly pleased that earlier this month Senator McCain led a congressional delegation to New Delhi, where he met with Prime Minister Modi.

Let me briefly touch on our U.S.-India Strategic Dialogue. Secretary Kerry is planning to travel to New Delhi later this month to cochair the U.S.-India Strategic Dialogue with his new counterpart, Minister of External Affairs Sushma Swaraj. This year, the Strategic Dialogue will highlight how U.S.-India ties promote shared prosperity in both countries.

We expect that the Strategic Dialogue will kick off a series of cabinet- and sub-cabinet-level visits throughout the late summer and fall, culminating in the visit of Prime Minister Modi to Washington at the invitation of the President.

Looking further out, we're particularly excited about the private sector-led U.S.-India Technology Summit, scheduled for November 2014 in the New Delhi area. The Tech summit—as we have dubbed it—will spur the formation of new partnerships between our countries in science-, technology-, and innovation-related sectors. We expect that our most successful American firms will participate, and we're confident large-scale events like this will help create jobs and build new partnerships in both countries.

Today, we see the U.S.-India relationship on increasingly sure footing. But with countries as large as ours and with democratic systems that foster debate and dissent, we're likely to have some disagreements. It is only natural. However, I can assure you that our systems are mature enough to address impediments with honesty and sincerity, and ensure that no one, isolated incident can jeopardize what we have built over three successive presidencies and between our 1.6 billion citizens.

For India and the Indo-Pacific region to live up to their potential, they must create societies that encourage strong and inclusive economic growth; one where the private sector and not government leads economic development. They must quell terrorism and counter violent extremism while at the same time advancing human dignity and protecting religious freedom. They must address barriers preventing women and minority groups from full political, economic, and social participation.

Mr. Chairman, simply put, the Obama administration firmly believes that if the United States and India can continue to grow our trade and investment relationship and further enhance our already strong strategic partnership, we and the world will be better off. By reenergizing the U.S.-India relationship now, we are making future generations of Americans and Indians safer and more prosperous, and we are helping strengthen stability in Asia and around the world.

Finally, I would be remiss not to acknowledge the strong support of the U.S. Congress and this committee in particular for the U.S.-India partnership. Many of the greatest accomplishments over the last decade were made possible by the advocacy and support of members of both Houses, and from both parties. I look forward to working closely with you as we embark on a new chapter of U.S.-India relations in the months and years to come.

Thank you, Mr. Chairman. I look forward to answering any questions that you and others from the committee may have.

Senator KAINE. Thank you, Secretary Biswal.

Dr. Searight.

STATEMENT OF AMY SEARIGHT, PH.D., DEPUTY ASSISTANT SECRETARY OF DEFENSE FOR SOUTH AND SOUTHEAST ASIA, U.S. DEPARTMENT OF DEFENSE, WASHINGTON, DC

Dr. SEARIGHT. Thank you for inviting me to be here today to participate in this timely hearing on a very important relationship. As you all know, the U.S. Government and the Department of Defense are committed to a long-term strategic partnership with India. We view India as a regional and emerging global power, as well as a provider of security and a strategic partner with shared interests, from the Indian Ocean to Afghanistan and beyond.

Defense relations continue to play a significant role in advancing the strategic partnership and we continue to make progress toward advancing United States-India defense cooperation to the point where it is both expected and routine across our multifaceted relationship. The bottom line is that we want India to have all of the capabilities it needs to meet its security demands and we want to be a strong partner in that effort.

Our policy in this area has not changed and remains part of our broader rebalance to the region. We continue to maintain strong military-to-military ties and are building a growing record on defense trade. This partnership requires effort and persistence on both sides, and as we look ahead we see that there are even more areas where the two of us can cooperate.

One of the pillars of our effort to build a strategic partnership with India on defense is to U.S.-India Defense, Trade, and Technology Initiative, or DTTI. Secretary Hagel when he was recently in Singapore for the Shangri-La Dialogue designated the Under Secretary of Defense for Acquisition, Technology, and Logistics, Mr. Frank Kendall, to be his lead for DTTI. Even as Under Secretary Kendall assumes this role, the Secretary himself will continue to play a very strong personal role in making sure of the success of this initiative.

Only 2 months into Prime Minister Modi's tenure, it already looks like we will have a very busy year. Under the auspices of DTTI, we are ready to move forward on a number of efforts, from coproduction and codevelopment proposals to procurement and sales. On the coproduction and codevelopment side, we have continued to identify forward-leaning proposals from United States industry for cooperative projects with India. Once the new government shows interest in proposals already offered, we will follow up.

We also remain supportive of finding ways to include industry leaders in existing official dialogues and will continue to look for opportunities to foster close ties between the United States and Indian defense sectors. We hope to see more joint partnerships take root, like we have seen between Lockheed Martin and Tata building C–130 components in Hyderabad.

We will also continue to advocate on behalf of U.S. industry for needed changes in the Indian system, such as continued reforms to their offset system, and we will continue to emphasize that we offer a transparent export system in foreign military sales. On foreign direct investment, we are very encouraged by the Modi government's proposal in the budget introduced last week to raise FDI caps in the defense sector to 49 percent.

DTTI alone does not fully capture the scope of our engagement with the Indian Government. There are a wealth of opportunities for engagement already scheduled for this year and more are expected. We are now at the point where we can look toward the horizon and decide where we want to take the relationship further. We will continue to hold close consultations with India on Afghanistan and regional security and will look for opportunities to work together as our presence in Afghanistan draws down post-2014.

India is currently participating right now in the Rim of the Pacific, or RIMPAC, 2014 exercise in Hawaii, where for the first time an Indian frigate has joined this large multilateral activity. And Japan will participate in Malabar this year, which is our largest bilateral naval exercise with India and is schedule to take place at the end of this month.

Secretary Hagel will be traveling to India in early August to discuss bilateral defense ties with Indian officials. Under Secretary Kendall is expected to travel with him, as will I. This trip will follow the State Department's strategic dialogue which, as Secretary Biswal mentioned, will be in New Delhi on July 31, but this trip will be our first opportunity to engage in a direct and meaningful way with India's new leadership on defense and security issues that matter to us both.

In addition, the 2005 New Framework for the U.S.-India Defense Relationship will be up for renewal in June 2015 and we are looking for opportunities to reinforce and potentially expand efforts under its guidelines. The framework was a breakthrough document and laid out the bilateral defense cooperation structure that we follow today. This year we have an opportunity to review our progress and set goals for the coming decade on where we want to take the relationship next.

Thank you very much again for this opportunity and I look forward to your questions.

[The prepared statement of Dr. Searight follows:]

PREPARED STATEMENT OF DR. AMY SEARIGHT

Thank you for inviting to me to be here today to participate in this very timely hearing.

OVERVIEW

As you all know, the U.S. Government, and the Department of Defense are committed to a long-term strategic partnership with India. We view India as a regional and emerging global power, as well as a provider of security and a strategic partner with shared interests from the Indian Ocean to Afghanistan and beyond.

Defense relations continue to play a significant role in advancing the strategic partnership, and we continue to make progress toward advancing U.S.-India defense cooperation to the point where it is both expected and routine across our multifaceted relationship. Bottom line: we want India to have all of the capabilities it needs to meet its security demands, and we want to be a strong partner in that effort.

Our policy in this area has not changed, and remains part of our broader rebalance to the region. We continue to maintain strong military-to-military ties and are building a growing record on defense trade. This partnership requires effort and persistence on both sides, and as we look ahead, we see that there are even more areas where the two of us can cooperate.

UPDATE ON THE U.S.-INDIA DEFENSE TRADE AND TECHNOLOGY INITIATIVE

One of the pillars of our effort to build a strategic partnership with India on defense issues is the U.S.-India Defense Trade and Technology Initiative (DTTI). Secretary Hagel designated the Under Secretary of Defense for Acquisition, Technology, and Logistics, Frank Kendall, as his lead for the DTTI at the Shangri-La Dialogue in June. Even as Under Secretary Kendall assumes this role, the Secretary will continue to take a personal interest in the success of this initiative.

Only 2 months into Prime Minister Modi's tenure, already it looks like we will have a very busy year. Under the auspices of DTTI, we are ready to move forward on a number of efforts, from coproduction/codevelopment proposals to procurement and sales.

As you recall, DTTI was formulated in recognition that we needed to find a better way for our two systems to work together and to ensure that in cases where we wanted to collaborate, bureaucratic hurdles could be surmounted. It has paved the way for increased private sector ties, science and technology cooperation, defense trade, and potential for coproduction/codevelopment.

Regarding export controls, we continue to review each dual-use and munitions export application on a case-by-case basis. DOD provides its recommended dual-use positions to the Department of Commerce and munitions positions to the Department of State. Over the past year and a half, India has succeeded in acquiring the vast majority of what it sought to obtain from U.S. industry, with DOD recommending approval of just over 90 percent of dual-use requests and about 95 percent of munitions requests.

On the coproduction/codevelopment side, we have continued to identify forward-leaning proposals from U.S. industry for cooperative projects with India. Once the new government shows interest in the proposals already offered, we will follow up. Positive indications from the Indian side on these proposals would go a long way in helping us maintain the Initiative's momentum, but we realize that the new government—not even 2 months old—may take some time in responding.

We remain supportive of finding ways to include industry leaders in existing official dialogues, and will continue to look for opportunities to foster closer ties between the U.S. and Indian defense sectors. We hope to see more joint partnerships take root, like we have seen between Lockheed Martin and Tata building C-130 components in Hyderabad.

We will also continue to advocate on behalf of U.S. industry for needed changes in the Indian system—such as continued reforms to their offset system—and continue to emphasize that we offer a transparent export system in foreign military sales. On foreign direct investment, we are very encouraged by the Modi government's proposal in the budget introduced last week to raise FDI caps in the defense sector to 49 percent.

WAY FORWARD

DTTI alone does not fully capture the scope of our engagement with the Indian Government. There are a wealth of opportunities for engagement already scheduled for this year, and more are expected. We are now at a point where we can look toward the horizon and decide where we can take the relationship further.

We will continue to hold close consultations with India on Afghanistan and regional security, and will look for opportunities to work together as our presence in Afghanistan draws down post-2014.

India is currently participating in the Rim-of-the-Pacific (RIMPAC) 2014 exercise in Hawaii, where for the first time an Indian frigate has joined this large multilateral activity. Japan will participate in MALABAR this year, our largest bilateral naval exercise with India, scheduled for the end of this month.

Secretary Hagel will be traveling to India in early August to discuss bilateral defense ties with Indian officials. Under Secretary Kendall is expected to travel with him, as will I. This trip will follow the State Department's Strategic Dialogue, scheduled for July 31 in New Delhi, and will be our first opportunity to engage in a direct and meaningful way with India's new leadership on defense and security issues that matter to us both.

We also look forward to convening the Defense Policy Group (DPG) this year, now that Under Secretary of Defense for Policy, Christine Wormuth, has been confirmed. As the premier defense dialogue between our two countries, it is extremely important for this group and its subgroups to be reenergized as we look toward a very busy year.

The 2005 New Framework for the U.S.-India Defense Relationship will be up for renewal in June 2015, and we are looking for opportunities to reinforce and potentially expand efforts under its guidelines. The Framework was a breakthrough document and laid out the bilateral defense cooperation structure we follow today. This year, we have an opportunity to review our progress and set goals for the coming decade on where we want to take the relationship next.

As we enter this window of opportunity on both sides, we need to ensure our bureaucracies do not prevent progress and further development of a vital strategic partnership. We will continue to urge both sides to keep moving forward, deepen our candor in discussions, and find new areas to collaborate in the coming years.

Thank you again for this opportunity, and I look forward to your questions.

Senator KAINE. Great. Thank you.

We will do questions in 6-minute rounds and I will begin. Secretary Biswal, dig in a little bit more to your recent visit with Deputy Secretary Burns. You talked about direct dialogue with Prime Minister Modi and his clarity about the priorities that he views as his most pressing priorities. If you could talk a little bit about that discussion and the kinds of priorities where he wants to focus his initial energies, that would be helpful.

Ms. BISWAL. Certainly. Thank you, Mr. Chairman. We did have a very good meeting with the Prime Minister, as well as with the Finance Minister, with the External Affairs Minister, and various other members of the Cabinet. Clearly the economic growth agenda is going to be one of the key agendas, and within that they have identified a desire for increased United States-India cooperation in infrastructure, in manufacturing, in the energy sector, and certainly looking at the whole issue of skills and how we can improve access to education and skills in terms of the Indian population.

Those are all areas where we think that American educational institutions and American businesses, American technology, bring very significant added value, and we are looking to see how we can address some of those areas in more specificity as we look forward to the strategic dialogue and to the Prime Minister's visit here this fall.

Senator KAINE. One of the initial signs that I thought was very positive was in Prime Minister Modi's inauguration, his decision to invite Pakistani Prime Minister Sharif, and not only to have him attend, as other heads of state did, but the opportunity that they took to then find time to speak together at some length. How do you see Indo-Pakistani ties today and how are they progressing? Can greater trade contribute to closer relationships and rapprochement in the region?

Ms. BISWAL. You know, Mr. Chairman, both Prime Minister Sharif and Prime Minister Modi have come into office with a very strong agenda and a very strong mandate for economic opportunity for their populations. We see an improvement and an opening in the economic relationship between India and Pakistan as one win-win opportunity that both leaders could and should pursue. We have seen some statements to that effect that make us think that such an easing of trade relations, improving of trade relations, is something that both are considering. So we would hope and we would encourage that this would be an important way to invest both countries in each other's economies and in each other's opportunities.

Senator KAINE. Thank you.

Dr. Searight, I was surprised as I was preparing for this hearing with staff to read—and just tell me if this is right—that the United States and India from a defense standpoint have as many joint exercises together as the United States has with any other nation in the world. The notion of this kind of joint activity is pretty significant.

I wanted to ask in particular about cooperation on counterterrorism strategies. The United States is dealing with it and India has dealt with it as well. Talk to me a little bit about the level of cooperation between us on counterterrorism activities?

Dr. SEARIGHT. Mr. Chairman, you are correct that we do a broad range of military-to-military activities, including a number of exercises. In terms of specific counterterrorism exercises, I will have to get back to you with the specifics on that.

Senator KAINE. How about, separate from exercises, just the state of the relationship on counterterrorism planning? Talk to me about that a little bit if you can, or Secretary Biswal, either way?

Ms. BISWAL. Sure. We have very extensive areas of cooperation on counterterrorism. It is both a priority for the United States and one for the Indian Government. So we have a homeland security dialogue where we do both discussions on intelligence cooperation with respect to counterterrorism and on technology and training and capacity issues with respect to counterterrorism. We expect that the strategic dialogue later this month will have a strong component focused on counterterrorism as well, with participation from the Department of Homeland Security, the State Department's Bureau of Counterterrorism, and other key players, to see how we can expand both the institutional aspects of cooperation as well as the operational aspects of cooperation.

Senator KAINE. Thank you very much.

One of the things we have been supportive of in the past has been Indian membership in multilateral export control regimes. There are four in particular where we have supported India's participation in: The Nuclear Suppliers Group, Missile Technology Control Regime, the Wassenaar Agreement, and the Australia Group. What is the current status of India progressing into membership in these multinational export regimes?

Ms. BISWAL. We continue to very much strongly support India's inclusion in those four regimes, and India has been taking steps in terms of its own aspirations and applications to those regimes. It is an issue where it is not solely up to the United States and we continue to look for opportunities to advance India's membership.

Senator KAINE. We have a U.S.-India Higher Education Dialogue that has a number of purposes, one of which is to try to deal with a system that has a tremendous demand. They are overburdened by the demand and the United States and India are cooperating in dealing with it. What is the current status of that U.S.-India Higher Education Dialogue?

Ms. BISWAL. This is a very important area of collaboration between our two countries. We hope to have a higher education dialogue later this year, both in terms of how we can expand access to American educational institutions for Indian students who are seeking to come to the United States and how we can expand opportunities for American institutions to partner with and provide opportunities in India.

There is a very strong emphasis on access to education for the new government as they look to increase the skills base of their work force and I think that there is an opportunity here as we look at things like community colleges and the systems that have worked so well in our country, how we can partner and collaborate to provide those kinds of educational platforms in India as well.

Senator KAINE. Great. Thank you.

Senator Risch.

Senator RISCH. Well, thank you.

Ms. Biswal, I want to go back to the matter I raised in my opening statement regarding civil nuclear power. As I explained, we are so proud of what we do in Idaho. We are the flagship—we have the flagship laboratory, the lead laboratory in America on civilian nuclear power. As a result of that, we do have relationships with other countries and we are proud of the relationship that we have with India, and particularly have the working group, and even going so far as to say it has been hosted there very recently.

But we are disappointed that we have been 6 years now and have not really seen the participation of the U.S. nuclear industry, in particular the companies being able to participate there. It of course surrounds this issue of liability. What can you tell us about that? What work is being done? What are the prospects? What is our prognosis for how that is going to resolve, if it is going to resolve?

Ms. BISWAL. Senator, we share your frustration in terms of the lack of progress over the last 6 years, while we did get some small progress and we were able to complete a small contract with respect to the previous government. We see some expanded areas of opportunity with the new government. While we have not yet had detailed discussions with the Modi government on the way forward on civil nuclear cooperation, we believe that there may be an opening to address nuclear liability issues either through a legal framework or through other frameworks that can help create more surety on what the application of liability might be, so that it is not unlimited liability, as the companies are rightly concerned.

But this is going to be an area that is going to require much greater discussion between the United States and India and between the companies and NPCIL to see what the way forward is going to be. I think that we have heard from Westinghouse that they think that there is a greater scope for trying to make progress on this and we are going to pursue that in the coming months.

Senator RISCH. I understand it is very early on in the Modi administration, but do you see some things there that give you some hope that there is going to be some movement in that regard?

Ms. BISWAL. We certainly heard statements that make us feel like there is a desire to find a way forward. The devil is always in the details and for that we really do need to wait and see what the conversations disclose.

Senator RISCH. Have you got any ideas or suggestions how we might move that forward a little by pushing a little bit on it?

Ms. BISWAL. Well, I think we need to see whether there are options either in terms of legislative remedies or regulatory remedies that can help create a framework for discussions to proceed with respect to liability. Beyond liability, there are a host of other issues that also need to be addressed, which we have not really been able to engage in until the liability issues are addressed.

Senator RISCH. Ms. Searight, next year the 10-year defense framework agreement expires. Do you have confidence we are going to be able to renegotiate that and get a new agreement to move forward?

Dr. SEARIGHT. Yes, that is certainly very high on our priority list. We do see it as a real opportunity to take stock of what we have accomplished under the framework agreement and sketch out where we would like to go. So this will be one of the things that Secretary Hagel will discuss with his counterparts when he visits India this August.

Senator RISCH. I assume from that statement that it is not moving forward yet, but you expect it to move forward soon?

Dr. SEARIGHT. Yes, we have not yet really engaged with this new Indian Government under Prime Minister Modi on renewing the framework agreement, but we have indicated our strong interest in doing so.

Senator RISCH. Have they reciprocated in that regard?

Dr. SEARIGHT. Yes, they have indicated that they are happy to hold those discussions.

Senator RISCH. Ms. Biswal, back to you on the intellectual property issue. Where are we headed in that direction with India? Has the new administration given us any signals that they understand the seriousness of this and the necessity that there be protections for intellectual property if we are going to do things right and move forward successfully?

Ms. BISWAL. As India seeks to develop the knowledge economy, it is going to need to grapple with this issue of intellectual property from the perspective even of indigenous innovation in India. I think that too often the discussion has been too much about what the United States thinks India ought to do, but intellectual property protection is fundamentally in India's own interest, and we think that Indian companies are increasingly making that fact known to the Indian Government.

So we think that as this government looks at its own economic agenda that strengthening and beefing up intellectual property protection in India is going to naturally emerge as an area of priority. We will continue to make that case with respect to the perspective of American companies and their ability to do business in India and to provide modern cutting-edge technology to India.

Senator RISCH. Referenced in your statement, kind of buried, was the statement that too often these are centered on what the United States thinks ought to be done. Is that a criticism that you hear, that we get regarding this issue?

Ms. BISWAL. No. I think that we are very compelling and forceful advocates of what we think is the right thing to do. But often what that is interpreted as is something where the United States thinks you ought to do this, and what is lost in the process is that this is actually what is necessary and right for India for its own agenda, for its own growth. I think we need to emphasize that these are things that India needs to do to be able to achieve its economic ambition.

Senator RISCH. I think with all countries sometimes you do not have the same—you know, our view of the intellectual property protection is based on personal property rights, which we as Americans seem sometimes to have a unique view of in the world. One of the things that has made us great is us having personal property rights; that we can accumulate and protect personal property.

Sometimes what you read, what you see from other countries, is they do not have the same view that intellectual property is personal property. I do not know how you bring people to the realization that intellectual property is property that has value just as much as currency or a bushel of wheat or anything else that is personal property that needs protection. What are your thoughts on that?

Ms. BISWAL. I think that that is a growing chorus that is heard within India, within the Indian private sector. I had the opportunity to meet with the head of NASSCOM, which represents kind of the technology sector in India, and I think that much of what we have articulated as being necessary for the investment climate—the business climate—in India to be attractive to American companies is also what the Indian private sector has also been articulating.

I think that when you have a government coming in with the mandate that this government has and with an outright majority and a very pro-business mind-set in terms of how to grow the economy, I think that we will see hopefully that some of these issues will have greater resonance.

Senator RISCH. Thank you very much, Mr. Chairman.

Senator KAINE. Thank you, Senator.

Senator McCain.

Senator McCAIN. Thank you. I thank the witnesses.

Ms. Biswal, it was my clear impression from meeting with the Prime Minister that he wants to focus our partnership on an ambitious strategic agenda. Would you generally agree with that?

Ms. BISWAL. That was certainly the impression we had as well in our conversation.

Senator McCAIN. What does the administration think the elements of that agenda might be?

Ms. BISWAL. We think that we have a very strong opportunity in terms of the security cooperation, the defense partnership, as Dr. Searight elaborated.

Senator McCAIN. What specifically would that be?

Ms. BISWAL. The Prime Minister in his conversation with us talked about defense manufacturing as a key area that India would like to pursue. We think that there is scope, and particularly, as Dr. Searight noted, the Indian budget did increase the FDI caps to 49 percent——

Senator McCAIN. I am not exactly sure that that is a strategic agenda.

Ms. BISWAL. But I think that as we have a greater collaboration in the defense partnership and in the security partnership that we also are going to advance our ability to work together around strategic objectives in the region, whether it is in terms of India's engagement in East Asia and working with us on issues of maritime security, whether it is in terms of India's engagement across South and Central Asia and the role that it plays. I think that that is one aspect of it.

We certainly look to increase our relationship with respect to how we are working together to address problems in the region and across the globe. I think that those are all areas that we need to strengthen the collaboration between our two countries.

Senator McCAIN. Strategic agenda? What is our overall strategy?

Ms. BISWAL. Senator, as you noted in your comments while you were in-country, we think that as India grows, as India prospers, and as India increases its capabilities, that India——

Senator McCAIN. No.

Ms. BISWAL [continuing]. As a partner in the region——

Senator McCAIN. Go ahead. But you still have not outlined the strategy. Strategy as I understand it are specific measures to ensure certain aspects of security. You have not mentioned China. You have not mentioned Japan. You have not mentioned that strategy and the threats that we are facing and the challenges that we are facing.

Ms. BISWAL. We have a very strong relationship and a trilateral partnership between the United States, India, and Japan. We were about to hold the fifth iteration of the U.S.-India-Japan Trilat earlier this summer. We have had to reschedule that, but we have seen a tremendous growth in the amount of collaboration that we are able to have, not only in terms of sharing of intelligence and analysis, but also looking at active areas of cooperation.

As Amy talked about, we will be doing joint exercises with Japan and India in the Malabar exercises later this fall. And we see opportunities for increasing the collaboration across Southeast Asia. We are engaging more frequently in consultations and dialogue with the Indians on ASEAN and look forward to increased and frequent consultations across the East Asia sphere.

We are also engaging in conversations with the Indians and consultations with respect to Afghanistan. With Deputy Secretary Burns we talked quite a bit about where things are headed and what role India can play in terms of the current electoral and political impasse in Afghanistan and how we can try to work together with respect to our objectives there.

But across the board, Senator, I think that the point that you are making, and we fully agree with, is that we have an opportunity here to engage more robustly with India in how the Asian landscape unfolds, and we look forward to engaging with this new government in that agenda.

Senator MCCAIN. I look forward to the articulation of a strategy.

Mrs. Searight—Dr. Searight, I am sorry. The Prime Minister of India, Prime Minister Modi, and Indian leaders are deeply concerned about President Obama's decision to fully withdraw United States troops from Afghanistan by January 2017 regardless of the conditions on the ground. Would you agree that that is generally the Indian position?

Dr. SEARIGHT. Yes, Senator McCain, I am aware that they have strong concerns. We do consult with them regularly on our Afghanistan policy and our plans for post-2014. Afghanistan is actually not in my purview, so for a more detailed answer I would have to get back to you.

Senator MCCAIN. But they are concerned about the situation in Afghanistan?

Dr. SEARIGHT. Yes, they are. And we very much appreciate their efforts to provide development assistance and training and support to Afghanistan forces.

Senator MCCAIN. Ms. Biswal, has the administration had any discussions with the government about Indian involvement in the TPP?

Ms. BISWAL. We have not yet been talking about Indian involvement in TPP, but we have talked to the Indians about what they see as their role in a global trade architecture. India itself has to make some decisions with respect to how it wants to open up its economy and engage in trade relations across Asia.

Senator MCCAIN. As you know, one of the big obstacles—problem areas that we have had—is on the nuclear issue with the Indians because of their legislation that basically makes it untenable for our nuclear capabilities to be sold to India. What do you think the answer to that problem is? They were saying that they thought that they could have new interpretation to government regulations rather than passing new legislation.

Do you think that that would be sufficient to satisfy the concerns of our manufacturers?

Ms. BISWAL. I think it is going to be up to the individual manufacturers to see what the level of assurance they need to feel comfortable. I think that if there is some combination of some regulatory along with, I think they have been talking about, insurance pools as well, that that might prove sufficient for some. But I think again that the companies are going to have to engage in these discussions, these negotiations, and see if there is a framework that will work for them.

Senator MCCAIN. Are you confident that that can happen?

Ms. BISWAL. I think we have to pursue this and see where it will go. I think that we see a willingness on the Indian side to enter into these conversations and to address the issue of liability, and we need to pursue that and see how far we can get there, get with that. I do think that it is a little bit premature right now because we have not had the detailed conversations to delve into exactly the specifics. But I think it is an opening that we are going to pursue and hopefully will be one aspect of the strategic dialogue coming up.

Senator McCain. Thank you.

Thank you, Mr. Chairman. I thank the witnesses.

Senator Kaine. Thank you, Senator McCain.

I actually want to follow up. Senator McCain raised a point about the India-China relationship. I would love to hear from each of you about this. It is a very important one. It has a bit of economic cooperation, but also strategic rivalry. I know there has been some recent visits with the new Prime Minister. Given the aggressive posture that China is showing on a number of areas, including maritime disputes, what is the concern level about potential tensions, either along the disputed border or Tibet or other issues that might be flashpoints, and what was the attitude that you found in Prime Minister Modi in talking about those issues?

Ms. Biswal. Clearly, there are going to be areas between India and China of economic collaboration and there will be areas of competition. I think that we want to see an India that is able to thrive and rise and we want to see that all of the economies of Asia are able to grow in a way that is sustainable and that mitigates against the areas of conflict.

With respect to the India-China relationship, I think you see that there will be areas where the United States and India will have great complementarity and collaboration and there will be areas where the United States and China will be working together, and there will be areas where India and China will be working together. I think that that is the era that we are walking into. A rising India is in some ways going to be an ameliorating influence on China, in China's own growth and in China's own behavior in the region.

Senator Kaine. Dr. Searight, from the defense standpoint?

Dr. Searight. Yes, thank you. As India looks east and we pursue our strategic rebalance, there is a real strategic convergence there as we both are looking to the challenges and opportunities in East Asia today, of which a rising China is certainly a major part. So India has integrated itself into the ASEAN-led regional architecture, as have we. So we are beginning to cooperate much more with India on the kind of work that we do in ASEAN-based organizations, such as, from the defense perspective what is important to us is the ASEAN Defense Ministers meeting, or ADMM-Plus framework.

The challenges that those kinds of frameworks address are things like maritime security. There are obviously a lot of tensions in the maritime domain in the region right now. So those are the areas where I think there are concerns on India's part, there are concerns on our part, there are concerns on many of the ASEAN nations' part. Those are the discussions we are having in those frameworks and having separately with India.

We have already mentioned a couple of times opportunities for trilateral cooperation with Japan. We have mentioned Malabar, that will be taking place off the coast of Okinawa later this month. USS *John S. McCain* will be participating in that exercise. So that is another example where there is a growing relationship between India and Japan, there is a growing relationship between India and ASEAN countries, Vietnam in particular. There is a new defense relationship growing there. We want to capitalize on that, and we do not have to be in all of the discussions with those partners, but we want to support that activity and participate trilaterally or multilaterally where it is appropriate.

Senator KAINE. One last question, Secretary Biswal, about sort of a diplomatic matter. The friction points—the Khobragade incident last year was a real friction point. These kinds of things will come up, but it almost seemed like the friction was more about the sort of communication and how it was handled than the initial incident, which could have been handled.

Have we learned anything from that, both the United States and India, in the aftermath of that? And can we put those lessons to use to avoid this kind of friction in the future?

Ms. BISWAL. Mr. Chairman, we have certainly spent many, many long hours discussing with our Indian colleagues ways to, one, ensure that we have greater understandings and greater clarity about our expectations of each other under each other's laws and under each other's systems. I think that that has been time well spent.

We have also focused a great deal on ensuring that we have more clear and transparent communication to ensure that we anticipate problems before they happen, that we clearly communicate those problems, and that we resolve them. So I think that, despite the fact that we had this very uncomfortable and unfortunate situation that we had to work through, at the end of the day I think we have developed closer ties and closer communications with our two systems as a result.

Senator KAINE. Then actually one more question. Talking about trilateral activities between the United States and India and Japan and then United States, India, and China within that trilateral, the United States and India may be complementary on some issues, China and India in some, United States-China in some. Are there trilateral opportunities. The United States-India-China is nearly half the world's population, half the world's economic output. What are the trilateral opportunities, if any, that we should be thinking about?

Ms. BISWAL. It has been an area that has been tossed around in various fora. I think right now we do have track-two opportunities where we have members of the think tank community, academia, from the three countries who engage in those conversations and I think it bears watching to see if it might be an opportunity to develop that into a track-one opportunity down the road.

Senator KAINE. Well, I would like to thank the witnesses on panel one for your testimony and again for your service. It is good to have you before us. I know Senators Risch and McCain join in the thanks. With that, we will move you aside for panel two. But thanks for being up with us today.

If I could ask the second panel to come forward. While they are, for the audience let me just introduce our second panel members. We have a superb lineup in panel two: Ambassador Frank Wisner, who is currently an international affairs adviser at the Patton Boggs firm, where he uses international experience to help clients with strategic global advice. As all know, Ambassador Wisner served as Ambassador to India from 1993 to 1997, also served as Ambassador to the Philippines, Egypt, and Zambia, and as Under

Secretary of Defense for Policy. Ambassador Wisner, it is good to have you with us.

Vikram Singh is vice president of National Security and International Policy at American Progress. Previously he served as Deputy Assistant Secretary of Defense for South and Southeast Asia at the Pentagon. Singh was also Deputy Special Representative for Afghanistan and Pakistan at the U.S. Department of State.

Richard ''Rick'' Rossow is the senior fellow and holds the Wadhwani Chair in U.S.-India Policy Studies at the Center for Strategic and International Studies. Prior to CSIS, Mr. Rossow spent 16 years working on a variety of capacities to strengthen the partnership between the United States and India.

Lisa Curtis. We are glad to have Lisa with us. She analyzes America's economic security and political relationships with India, Pakistan, and Afghanistan and other nations in South Asia as a senior research fellow at the Heritage Institute. Before joining Heritage in 2006, Ms. Curtis was a member of the professional staff of the Senate Foreign Relations Committee. Welcome back. It is good to have you on that side of the table.

I will start with Ambassador Wisner and then we will just move across the table for each of your testimony, and then we will open it up for questions. As I say, I do expect Senator Risch will return. Ambassador Wisner, welcome.

STATEMENT OF HON. FRANK G. WISNER, FOREIGN AFFAIRS ADVISOR, SQUIRE PATTON BOGGS, WASHINGTON, DC

Ambassador WISNER. Senator, thank you very much. It is an honor to appear before your subcommittee. I, like the others who have gathered with me, will submit my formal testimony for the record.

Senator KAINE. Absolutely.

Ambassador WISNER. Instead, what I thought I might do is think out loud for a few minutes about the Indian-American relationship and how we might best advance it. In this regard, I would like to make five points.

The first is pretty obvious and it springs from your testimony, your statement, and that is that India is truly important to the United States. It is important to us because India helps assure a balance of power in Asia in a time in which American interests in the most fundamental fashion will be challenged as we move increasingly into a Pacific century.

The same is true in the opposite side. We are vitally important to India. We are India's best market for technology, for trade, for defense cooperation. We are on the other side of the equation of balance. A strong India is good for America, a strong America is, in like manner, good for India.

If you start with that point, then the next should follow. That is you can argue the United States and India could have done more with their relationship in recent years, but let us also remember that we have taken gigantic steps. A real sea change has occurred in the last 15 to 20 years in the way we have dealt with each other.

Having said that, I truly believe that since 2010, the high water marked by President Obama's trip, the relationship has been on hold. If anything, I would say it has atrophied and requires attention.

Which is my third point, and that is the unprecedented victory of Prime Minister Modi, the disarray of the opposition, the determination of Modi to shape the agenda of his country, means that the United States is facing an uncommon partner across the table, an uncommon opportunity, and one that is likely to be with us for a good 10 years. We should be planning that the partners we have in New Delhi today will be there for a substantial period of time. It behooves us therefore to make certain that we get the relationship right, our understandings right, now, so that we have the enduring capacity to engage India in the years ahead.

My fourth point flows therefore from that, and it is: What are the main pillars of the relationship and how do we address those? I am going to argue that at core the relationship has rested on two pillars since it took off in its modern phase in the 1990s. The first is political. We have developed a new political relationship with India in the past decade and a half that is unlike anything that we have known before in our history.

But I am also going to argue that since 2010 we have begun to lose the strategic thread in that relationship. I believe that is the point Senator McCain was driving this afternoon. What is the strategic view? How do we see India and therefore how does India judge where she fits into American strategy, especially at a time when India is trying to calibrate its relations with China, Pakistan, Afghanistan, and the other crises in the region. Where India fits in is going to be the basis of how Modi and his government decide to structure their national policies and develop a partnership with the United States.

Now, it is more than general generalities. It is very specific. How does the United States intend to manage the rise of Chinese power? What does the United States intend to do with, and in, Afghanistan after the withdrawal of American forces in their great majority in 2014? Under what circumstances are we going to come to the assistance of Afghanistan or back the existing regime? How will India be able to relate to our objectives?

And third, Pakistan. While India brooks no intermediation between the United States and Pakistan, India still needs to know how we will deal with the very difficult circumstances Pakistan is going through and the spillover effect across India's borders.

I believe, Senator, that these three particular questions and the broader strategic framework must be the top priority of Secretary Kerry and the President when Prime Minister Modi visits the United States in September.

I believe it is also a challenge for this committee to think how to articulate American strategic purposes in Asia and toward India, as well as Japan and China. That remains a real task in front of all of us.

I think we saw this afternoon the need to refine our thinking so that we can create partners in our activities abroad.

The second aspect of our relationship, the second pillar, Senator Kaine, is the economic pillar. It has been a real driver in what got us here. In the last 4 or 5 years, there has been a loss of confidence in the American business community in the Indian market. India has not grown rapidly. GDP rates have been down, inflation high, and government has not been able to take the steps which are necessary to push the relationship forward or, indeed, resume a high rate of Indian growth.

Reversing that tide is the top priority in the Modi government, and it is also the top priority we have on the business side. There are lots of issues that have to be dealt with. Some have been mentioned this afternoon: questions of taxes, of intellectual property rights. I believe there are avenues forward. The nuclear question we have touched on. Defense sales and offsets; the Indian threat, occasionally voiced, of localization; the criminalization of commercial disputes that has today an American CEO in prison in an eastern Indian state, the Amway president; the long-term difficulties of infrastructure and power generation which impede the effectiveness of American business firms which invest or which wish to trade from and produce in India.

Modi, the Prime Minister, intends to address these issues. He made that clear and his government made it clear to the delegation that visited India in late June from the United States-India Business Council headed by Chairman Ajay Banga. The USIBC represents the overwhelming majority of American companies doing business in India. The Prime Minister made it absolutely clear that we would see first steps in a new budget. While I conclude we have not seen a lot of hard facts in the budget, we have seen key directions and that is very important.

Modi made it clear he wants to produce 15 million jobs a year and he knows, and his government knows, you cannot get there without foreign involvement, foreign investment, foreign technology, and without American involvement.

Well, growth of the Indian economy is going to be good for us. It is going to be important for India. But I am going to take the argument one step further since you and this subcommittee want to look ahead. Where do we want to be in the future? Where does India want to be? How will it develop 15 million jobs?

I argue that the only way there is a real shot at getting to that goal is for India to open itself up and become a competitive marketplace for trade and investment in the international system. Yes, as Assistant Secretary Biswal said, we would like to see the bilateral investment treaty passed. That is an important objective. We want to see India back in the WTO engaging in the service rounds. It is really important to see India in APEC and looking at the Trans-Pacific Partnership, and indeed one day, Senator, perhaps we can dream, if we can take those initial steps, of a free trade agreement between the United States and India.

For India today finds itself in the awkward position of being neither part of the Atlantic disposition nor the Pacific one and falling in between. But for India to reach the objective of an open and competative trade and investment regime takes a mind-set change. Will India open up? Rather than investment only flowing in, is India ready to join the international trading system and establish best investment practices.

I believe it is important. I believe it is part, circling back to Senator McCain, of the strategic challenge. Do we want to leave India struggling at the door of APEC, trying to figure out how to get in?

Or do we, the United States, want to be India's partner in trying to help her think through the steps she will have to take?

So political strategy and business come together again.

For all of these things to happen, there are a number of fora. The Secretary and the Secretary of Commerce will be in Delhi. The President will be involved. Many other fora have been mentioned. They need to be launched, because we have real jobs to do.

But I close by saying, Senator, that we really have an extraordinary opportunity with India and a demanding time in which to make that opportunity happen. I believe today and I believed for some time that, despite the progress we have made so far, the best years in our relationship are still to come.

[The prepared statement of Ambassador Wisner follows:]

PREPARED STATEMENT OF AMBASSADOR FRANK G. WISNER

Senator Kaine and Senator Risch, it is an honor to appear before your subcommittee and address the important question of ''Indispensable Partners: Reenergizing U.S.-India Ties.''

I come to these proceedings with experience in dealing with U.S.-India relations. I served as United States Ambassador in New Delhi from 1993–1997. I have chaired the U.S.-India Business Council and at present I am a member of its Board of Directors and its Executive Committee. Since leaving government service, I have participated regularly in fora which bring together Indian and American experts in public policy. I have also authored or participated in a variety of study groups which address the Indian American relationship. My professional obligations take me to India regularly and I returned from India in late June of this year, where together with a delegation from the U.S. India Business Council, I met members of the new government and leaders in the Indian business community.

In my testimony, I intend to address the state of the U.S.-India relationship and what needs to be done to give it fresh energy and importance to our two countries.

Before turning to this subject, I admit to being biased. I believe a strong U.S.-India relationship is good for the United States and the opposite is true as well. American strength in the world and prosperity at home are important to India, just as a secure and prosperous India benefits the United States. I have held these opinions firmly over nearly 20 years, despite the ups and downs in the Indian-American relationship. My reasons are simple. India is an emerging global power. Its weight is felt particularly in Asia where India plays a pivotal role in maintaining the balance of power among Asia's great nations. India is coming into its own as a major international economic player whose trade with the United States means that India will be a valuable market for the exports of American goods and services as well as a source of two way investment and technology exchange for years to come. In a word, we need close political and economic ties to India. It is a nation with which we share common values, especially democratic ones. We also are a home to a large, productive community of Americans of Indian origin.

It is on these common interests that our relationship with India has developed over the past quarter century. The strength of our political and economic relations with India have regrettably atrophied over the last 4 years and need attention if we are to set a stronger basis for our relationship and more effectively pursue our respective national interests. At the heart of the challenge is a strategic question. On our side we lost confidence in the last Indian Government's ability to follow through with the undertakings we believe it made to us and to find common ground with us on a number of questions—trade being a notable example. The relationship took on the tone of a transactional undertaking. On the Indian side, many argue they do not understand American strategy in Asia, including in South Asia. They thought they understood the Bush administration's approach to the continent's security problems, especially our approach to China. They assert they have found no comparable clarity in the Obama administration's views. Indians wish to understand our strategy for a good reason. They want to know their place in it. The definition will permit the Indian Government to make its choices.

Indians are especially concerned with how the United States intends to deal with the rise of Chinese power. This Indian Government, like its predecessor, sees China as its principal, long-term strategic and economic competitor. India fought a war with China; it has unresolved border issues with China; its economic relationships are filled with points of friction. India's defense posture is heavily dictated by the potential threat from China. And India's new ties with Japan reflect Indian pre-occupations with China. How does the U.S. intend to cope with China's rise is the lead question on Indian minds.

Indians also follow events in Afghanistan closely and believe that Afghanistan's fate directly affects India's security. Indian officials want to know how we plan to proceed after the withdrawal of American and NATO troops; how we will be engaged in supporting the Kabul regime and what steps we have in mind to keep the Taliban at bay. Across the border, Indians watch with growing concern deteriorating conditions in Pakistan and are directly threatened by the actions of the Pakistani Government and rogue radical terrorist across India's boarders. Pakistani origin terror and involvement in Kashmir remain major questions for India.

Prime Minister Modi has opened a dialogue with Pakistan's Prime Minister. He and his colleagues do not seek American mediation nor direct involvement. Indians believe they can find their own way forward with Pakistan and that American involvement will complicate the ability of the two governments to manage their differences. Instead the Indian Government looks to us for encouragement and with respect to Pakistan, the Indians expect us to be clear what the steps we will take to nudge Pakistan toward a peaceful relationship with India.

Our current strategic dialogue contains many channels for discussing political, intelligence and security matters. Our military exercises and defense trade strengthen our ability to deal with India's national security establishment. But these activities need a strategic definition and that is the task before Secretary Kerry when he visits India this month. It is also the challenge the President will face when he meets Prime Minister Modi in September in Washington. It is important that we get our strategic definition right. Prime Minister Modi's recent election is virtually unprecedented; he comes to office with great authority; the opposition is in disarray and will be so for sometime to come. We are wise to assume that the Prime Minister and his party may be in office for the next 10 years. It is a good time to define our political and security relationship.

In defining national strategy, I believe your committee can play a key role and take part in the strategic dialogue between our two countries. I urge through these hearings and others like them and through your visits to India that you do so.

The second pillar in our relationship with India is business. Our commercial and investment interests with India also need attention. In the 1990s, the engagement of the American business community in India was the driving force in the relationship. In recent years, American business has lost confidence in the Indian market. Indian rates of growth have slowed and the Indian Government's restrictions on foreign ownership, its tax policies, approaches to intellectual property rights, its insistence on localization, the criminalization of civil disputes that has put an American CEO in jail, and failed attempts to secure legislation which would permit American investment in the nuclear power industry are all examples of why American companies have backed away from the Indian market. These issues must be addressed if there is to be renewed American investor confidence in India.

This said, Prime Minister Modi's government has sent a strong signal that it intends to be business friendly. In my judgment, India's Government will address individual business problems American enterprises face, as well as the policies which lay behind them. Unlike its predecessor the Modi government is principally about growth. Its first budget, announced on July 10, signals new policy directions— a determined effort to strengthen India's weak public finances, tackle inflation, revive the sluggish economy and build an investor friendly environment. The budget also addresses two issues of great importance to the United States—increased foreign ownership in the defense and in the insurance industries.

Prime Minister Modi seeks investment in India. He wants to create 15 million new jobs a year. The challenge is enormous and he believes it can only be met in partnership with foreign, including American, enterprise. He will succeed if the business policies he sponsors create an atmosphere of predictability, consistency, and transparency.

I believe that his ambition can best be met if he commits India to a more robust free trade and investment regime. I also am persuaded that our economic relationship with India needs a long-term objective which will drive action and capture imagination. Free trade and investment are precisely the right sort of priorities, for they bring reciprocal benefits to India and to the United States. This said, we have a long road to travel before we can reach a free trade destination. First, we need to complete our Bilateral Investment Treaty; we need India's reengagement in WTO negotiations. Further along, India has a choice to make about APEC and the Trans-Pacific trading regime. But we have a decision to make as well. We can let India struggle on its own or we can turn Indian interest in Pacific trade into a strategic feature in our relationship. Finally, and at a future point in our history, we and India might set our sights on a bilateral free trade agreement.

Free Trade and investment are important objectives. India should not let itself fall between the emerging Atlantic and Pacific trading regimes. But a commitment to freer trade and investment implies a tough choice for India. Is India ready to enter the world trading system wholeheartedly or is it more concerned about attracting investment and trade to its shores, protecting itself from international competition? I believe the first choice is the surer way to Indian prosperity and national economic strength.

The United States and India have a variety of public and private fora to discuss trade and investment issues. Several, like the Trade Policy Forum, has lapsed and need to be reenergized. These institutions are part of the fabric of the U.S.-India relationship. However, they only find their logic when we and India agree on policy objectives which benefit both nations. Neither we nor India will ever achieve all of our objectives. Building the relationship calls for patience, forbearance, and for give and take; it also calls for determined action. Neither India nor the United States will accept dictation or pressure. If we handle our relationship with respect, the rewards are significant. India can emerge as one of this country's major strategic and economic partners and in turn, we can help India strengthen India's security and promote the welfare of its people. We both need that sort of relationship in our troubling and demanding world

I appreciate the subcommittee's attention to my arguments and I am open for questioning.

Senator KAINE. Thank you, Mr. Ambassador.

Mr. Rossow.

STATEMENT OF RICHARD M. ROSSOW, WADHWANI CHAIR IN U.S.–INDIA POLICY STUDIES, CENTER FOR STRATEGIC AND INTERNATIONAL STUDIES, WASHINGTON, DC

Mr. ROSSOW. Chairman Kaine, Ranking Member Risch, first, let me also offer my sincere thanks for organizing this hearing. The title and tenor differs greatly from what we saw around Washington, DC, and the Hill just a year ago, when some troubling economic policies in India really tended to dominate our bilateral agenda.

Commercial issues are real and quite serious and have been touched on already several times. But let us first remember, as has already been said, why partnership with India is important. I think every time that we see a fishing boat rammed in the South China Sea, I think every single time that an air defense identification zone is set up without consultation, every time that an island is created in the middle of the ocean attempting to expand territorial claims, we understand why we need strong regional partners. So I think the conversation here is quite timely with the election.

This belief drove the United States to make an initial attempt at creating a powerful new partnership with India over a decade ago, highlighted most poignantly by the United States-India civilian commercial deal. However, the last Indian Parliament gutted the commercial aspects of this deal by passing the liability law that has been touched upon. At that point we really had to question India's commitment to a strategic partnership.

At that time we kind of fell back on commercial relations as really the driver of bilateral affairs, and when these economic policy decisions were taken even that fell off the rail. So that is where we started.

There is a very different leadership team in Delhi now, though. The BJP is not guided by India's traditional history of nonalignment. They have only been in charge in 6 of India's years since independence. So the past is not precedent for them. Instead of standing on lofty principles, which may in fact be at odds with their circumstances, the Modi government will strike out in bold new directions which meet specific goals.

My good friend, Ambassador Hemant Singh, said the other day when he came through town: India's actions will finally be aligned with her priorities. I think that captured it most poignantly.

My biggest fear is the United States, both government and industry, suffer from failed expectation syndrome right now. Not everyone on our side of the ocean seems to understand the sea change in Delhi and how this could serve to deepen our partnership. We may not be prepared to make a second grand overture, as we did in the past, or be receptive should India signal its interest in striking out in bold new directions.

My second fear is that we will approach the Modi government with the same agenda that we have used in recent years. We need to recognize the Modi government's priorities, some of which have been discussed already today, and where these priorities intersect with our own, and this middle ground must become our shared agenda.

So four areas that I would point to: First is manufacturing, which has already been touched on. Ambassador Wisner noted the need for 15 million jobs a year to be created. The other aspect on manufacturing: Almost 100 million people have moved to Indian cities in the last 10 years, and India's trade deficit, particularly with China, of about $40 billion—they need to come up with opportunities and means to back those issues off and create opportunities for themselves. America can be a crucial partner in manufacturing, supplying capital equipment, financing, investment, and markets for the redevelopment of the Indian manufacturing sector.

Second is on defense. Clearly this remains the brightest area of United States-India cooperation, but I will leave that for Vikram as the expert here. Internal security, border incident, or terror incident—most of us look at that in the Modi tenure as one of the biggest threats to derailing Modi's governance over the next 5 years— another Mumbai-style attack and the feeling that he will have to react more forcefully than the Manmohan Singh government did.

Here again, the United States has a great deal to offer on internal security, from equipment to intelligence-sharing, and this must include a much more collaborative approach on Afghanistan as we shape our planning for Afghanistan, not just telling them what we are going to do, but at least bringing them in the loop earlier in that process.

Creating infrastructure. This is the fourth area that the Modi government is very interested in. Actually, I think that there is a little bit less opportunity for American involvement in this, though. As Ambassador Wisner vividly recalls, a lot of the early American investment after the reforms in the 1990s were in the energy sector, power plants built across India, and had a difficult time getting paid. So whether there is a real opportunity for America to get back involved in infrastructure depends on whether we can find a payment security mechanism to make sure our companies get paid. The investment treaty could actually go some way in making that happen. So infrastructure, I hope that there is more to be done there.

When it comes to economic cooperation, Washington spends a great deal of time talking about liberalization as the thing that will unleash the animal forces. To be sure, increasing FDI caps will provide much-needed capital to spur additional growth in sectors like insurance, retail trade, defense, and a range of other industries. But even if nothing that we call reform happens in India, the biggest reform has already happened, which is having a business-friendly government in charge in Delhi.

Running a clean and fair spectrum allocation for telecom spectrum may not qualify as a reform, but if this Modi government is able to do it it will be an important boost of the telecom industry and for Internet penetration. Avoiding regulatory overreach would not qualify perhaps as liberalization, but it can avoid the collapse of an industry, as we saw with the life insurance industry in India in 2010, with the regulatory change that really gutted the growth rate of one of the fastest growing industries at the time.

So business can operate in most environments as long as there is stable, consistent application of the rules, and that has not been the case in recent years. So we look at reforms, but I think the numbers are going to show that, irrespective of whether the FDI caps change—and I certainly hope they do—I think business is going to be a lot more bullish, and we are seeing the numbers tip up already.

The last time the BJP was in power, in less than 6 years we went from nuclear sanctions to nuclear cooperation—6 years. When interests are aligned and leaders think big, the relationship can progress faster than most of us believe is possible. This Indian Government is not bound by precedents. The reasons for partnership with India are stronger now than they were a decade ago, and America needs to approach these next 2 months without putting a ceiling on how big we are thinking and without the baggage of the last 5 years.

I thank you for your time.

[The prepared statement of Mr. Rossow follows:]

PREPARED STATEMENT OF RICHARD M. ROSSOW

Chairman Kaine, Ranking Member Risch, members of the committee, first let me offer my sincere thanks for organizing this hearing. The title and tenor differs greatly from what we saw from around Washington, DC, and the Hill last year when a small group of companies with serious concerns about economic policies in India dominated our bilateral agenda.

The issues these companies raised are real and serious. But let us first remember why a strong India—and a deep partnership with India—is in our national interest. A large, democratic nation with similar values in that region will be a stabilizing force. Every time a fishing boat is rammed in Asia, an Air Defense Identification Zone is created over disputed territory without consultation, or an island is constructed in the middle of the sea to expand territorial claims—we are reminded of the need for strong regional partners.

This belief drove the United States to make its initial attempt at creating a powerful new partnership with India over a decade ago. This partnership was illustrated most vividly by the U.S. India Civilian Nuclear Agreement. However, when the last Indian Parliament gutted the commercial meaning of the deal by approving a weak nuclear liability law, we had to question India's commitment to a deeper partnership. U.S.-India relations relied once more on commercial ties. Even this aspect of the relationship became strained when the Indian Government introduced a series of stopgap policy measures meant to shore up voter support ahead of this year's election.

Now there is a very different team in New Delhi. The BJP is not guided by India's traditional policy of nonalignment. Instead of standing on lofty principles which may, in fact, be at odds with her circumstances, the Modi government will strike out in bold new directions which meet specific goals.

My biggest fear is that the United States—both government and industry—suffer from "failed expectation syndrome." Not everyone on our side of the ocean seems to understand the sea change in Delhi, and how this could serve to deepen our partnership. We may not be prepared to make a second "grand overture," or be receptive should India signal its interest in bold new ideas.

My second fear is that we will approach the Modi government with the same agenda we used in recent years. We need to recognize the Modi government's priorities, and where these priorities intersect with our own. This middle ground must become our shared agenda.

Four areas are emerging as particularly important to the Modi government.

1. *Creating infrastructure*. India is amazingly deficient in infrastructure. Frankly speaking, the U.S. will not likely play a big role in building out India's infrastructure unless we conclude the BIT or find another payment security mechanism. India needs long-term capital willing to take certain risks that are not always a good match for American investors and developers.

2. *Manufacturing*. India desperately needs to create a stronger industrial base, to cut its trade deficit—which is far larger than America's as measured as a percent of GDP—and to provide opportunities for its fast-growing urban population. America can be a crucial partner, supplying capital equipment, financing, investment, and markets.

3. *Defense*. Clearly this remains the brightest area of U.S.-India cooperation. Next year our Defense Framework Agreement expires; renewal—and possible expansion—should be a priority. In addition, commercial defense relations will continue to thrive—especially if India liberalizes its offset and foreign investment rules.

4. *Internal security*. A terror or border incident involving Pakistan ranks among the biggest threats to Modi's agenda. India is very worried that the U.S. drawdown in Afghanistan will heighten the chances of an incident. The U.S. has a great deal to offer on internal security, from equipment to intelligence-sharing. This includes a more collaborative approach to engage New Delhi as we shape our planning for Afghanistan.

When it comes to economic cooperation, in Washington we spend a great deal of time talking about "liberalization" as the key to increasing American trade and investment. To be sure, increased FDI caps will provide much-needed capital to spur additional growth in insurance, retail trade, defense, and a range of other industries.

But even if nothing we call "reform" takes place, economic ties are going to get a great deal better. The biggest "reform" has already happened, through the election of a business-friendly government.

Running a clean and fair spectrum auction may not qualify as a "reform," but it would give an important boost to the telecommunications industry and for Internet penetration. Avoiding regulatory overreach is not "liberalization," but can avoid the collapse of an industry as we saw with life insurance regulatory changes in 2010. Business can operate in most environments so long as there is stable, consistent application of the rules—which has not been the case in recent years.

The last time the BJP was in power, in less than 6 years we went from nuclear sanctions to nuclear cooperation. When interests are aligned and leaders think big, the relationship can progress faster than most of us believe is possible.

This Indian Government is not bound by precedence.

The reasons for strategic partnership with India are stronger now than they were a decade ago.

America needs to approach these next 2 months without putting a ceiling on how big we are thinking, and without the baggage of the last 5 years.

Senator KAINE. Thank you very much.

Mr. Singh.

STATEMENT OF VIKRAM J. SINGH, VICE PRESIDENT, NATIONAL SECURITY AND INTERNATIONAL POLICY, CENTER FOR AMERICAN PROGRESS, WASHINGTON, DC

Mr. SINGH. Thank you very much, Mr. Chairman, Ranking Member Risch. It is a real honor to be here. As the other witnesses have done, I am submitting my testimony for the record as well, but I will touch on a few key areas briefly here which are going to echo a lot of what we have heard from my esteemed colleagues.

It really is a pleasure to be with you and this hearing could not be better timed. We are looking toward the moment that will set the trajectory for the next several years, with the strategic dialogue coming up, with the high-level visits we are going to have, and with the Prime Minister and the President meeting. So I am very glad to have the opportunity and to have it now. Thank you for that.

Interestingly, we are in virtually complete alignment with India on almost every major issue you could think about, at least in terms of where we want to go strategically. Terrorism, the environment, regional stability, counterproliferation. We agree that we need to have an international order based on rules and norms of behavior. We want secure energy flows, we want secure commerce. We want to combat global climate change. At home we have a lot of similar challenges. We face challenges in terms of the growth of the middle class and good jobs and providing good governance, protecting our citizens, securing energy and water for the future.

Our administrations, the current administration, the prior United States administration, successive Indian administrations for quite a while, have made this relationship a central priority. And yet we have found that progress has fallen short of expectations. Even where we have had breakthroughs—defense, the civil nuclear deal—it is important to note that we have given ourselves a good foundation, but we have lacked measurable progress in terms of deals signed, projects launched, joint activities undertaken.

There are some reasons for this, but we cannot gloss over them. There is a tendency in the United States-India relationship to have a little too much happy talk and then it is followed by excessive frustration. The bottom line is we are doing well, we are doing well together, and we could continue to do well together and be just fine, but we also have the potential in the next few years, we believe, at the Center for American Progress, we have the potential in the next few years to really move to another level in this relationship.

We are launching a project in the next week called India: 2020, which is going to look specifically at what can we do, and what can we achieve in 5 years, because we think this is a particularly good moment to look at that.

Prime Minister Modi ran on a campaign of what he called "Surajya," which means in Hindi good governance. He said: I am going to deliver good governance, I am going to deliver it to all classes, castes, and communities. That is the promise that he is going to be measured by. That is the promise that we should welcome and we should sort of measure him by ourselves.

I know he has been a controversial figure, but I really do think that the warmth of his reception in the United States this fall is critical. We need to set the tone now. This is the world's largest democracy and I think the Congress should invite him to a joint meeting. If the logistics work out, I think that needs to happen.

To evaluate how things are going in the first few days of the Modi administration, I think we should look at the budget. The budget is a good first step, but it showed that he views his challenges as long term and it was a set of incremental steps. It was not a sea change. You saw some increases in foreign direct investment. You saw some commitments to things like smart cities and infrastructure upgrades, but these were not met by commitments of resources. So we really are in a period of seeing just how ambitious and how fast the Modi government is going to move.

On defense, there are some near-term things that can be done to sort of show intent. There are pending sales, things like Apaches, Chinooks, the M777 howitzer. Those could all be done very soon. They could be done in time for Secretary Hagel's visit in August that we just heard about from Dr. Searight.

But there are longer things. That defense cooperation agreement she mentioned, the 2005 New Framework for Defense Cooperation is the agreement that governs this relationship. It has hit its 10-year mark. It was drafted as a 10-year agreement. It needs to be updated in a way that takes the vision for our security relationship to the next level. It should be updated to incorporate agreements for better communication and information-sharing and logistics cooperation, so that it actually enables us to do much more.

On economic liberalization, which was one of the areas you asked us to touch on, Modi is focused on this because India ranks 134th in the World Bank's "Doing Business" index. They have got a long way to go. I think it is good that we see the progress being made, but, to touch on what Ambassador Wisner said, issues like retroactive taxation, protection of intellectual property rights, the always emerging issues of local content requirements that have done things like made it very difficult for us to make progress even on renewable energy cooperation, those things need to be clarified and really clearly clarified. Some of these issues need to be put to bed by the Indian government if they are going to really attract the kind of investment it is going to take to have the kind of growth they want to see.

On energy and climate, we could do tremendous amounts together. India is going to be the world's largest coal consumer in a decade. India is already one of the largest emitters and it suffers great threat from climate change. So we could enhance cooperation in research and development. We could work together to reduce hydrofluorocarbons. We could build resilience, climate resilience. Our experience with Hurricane Sandy is very instructive. And we could model something on what we have done with them in terms of clean energy cooperation for building resilience and dealing with climate change.

But it is going to take a significant effort to get there, and we would have to clear away some of the things that have been real obstacles. So in the energy sector, their energy mix has got to include natural gas, nuclear, and other things. How far can we get if we do not resolve—or address the nuclear liability issue? Those are difficult issues, but they have to be grappled with. I think the new administration in India is going to give us an opportunity to do that.

I know everyone has talked a lot about the importance of India in the world and the region. I just want to say very briefly that I think it is important for us to start thinking about India as the anchor of a strategically vital part of the world, not as peripheral to South Asia or as peripheral to the Asia-Pacific, but as the anchor of the region that goes from the Middle East all the way to China, Japan, Australia, with India sitting in the center of it.

Modi has made very positive steps, sent positive indications about what he is going to do. He invited all the neighbors to his inauguration. He is going to continue to help contribute to stability in Afghanistan. He has made indications that he is going to take steps to improve stability with Pakistan if he can find a good counterpart.

We can work with them in the rest of the region—Nepal, Bangladesh, Sri Lanka. But also, for Myanmar, where India is working on connectivity, to new cooperation with Japan and Australia, which are areas that Modi seems to be interested in. He has shown that he wants to have good relations with China, but on the campaign trail he was also willing to actually publicly say China should not be an expansionist power, but should be focusing on development, which indicates that he is going to have a willingness to take on tough issues.

I think that the United States-India relationship has grown well, quietly, stably, in many ways. If you had said 10 or so years ago to me that we would have $10 billion in defense trade, I would have thought that was not even within the realm of possibility. But we have gotten there, and we should not rest on our laurels. I think the leadership of this committee and the opportunity before us, with new leadership in New Delhi, means that we are in a position to really capitalize on an opportunity and to take the relationship to the next level.

I look forward to the discussion. Thank you.

[The prepared statement of Mr. Singh follows:]

PREPARED STATEMENT OF VIKRAM J. SINGH

Chairman Kaine, Ranking Member Risch, members of the subcommittee, it is an honor to be with you today to discuss ''Reenergizing U.S.-India Ties.'' As Vice President for National Security and International Policy at the Center for American Progress, I see the U.S.-India relationship as one of the most critical priorities for our country. The timing of this hearing could not be better, with a new government in place in New Delhi, the fifth Strategic Dialogue scheduled for the end of the month, and President Obama meeting Prime Minister Modi in September.

All of you on the subcommittee and many members in the India Caucus have been vital to advancing the U.S.-India partnership. I'm pleased to be here with my dear friend and mentor, Ambassador Frank Wisner, along with two esteemed experts Richard Rossow and Lisa Curtis. I know you have also just heard from two true friends of this relationship, Assistant Secretary Biswal and Deputy Assistant Secretary Searight who succeeded me at the Pentagon.

Today I will touch briefly on each area you have highlighted, with special emphasis in areas in which I have the most experience: defense, security, and the Asia-Pacific region.

Since the end of the cold war and the launch of economic reforms in India in the early 1990s, the United States and India have lived with a permanent sense of expectation. It seems that the world's oldest and largest democracies are always on the cusp of becoming true strategic partners. The relationship has gained strong support across party lines in both countries. Cold-war-era gaps in trust have faded even through periods of significant tension, and by every objective measure—increased trade and investment, collaboration on regional and global security, people-to-people ties—we are closer than ever. Successive Indian and U.S. administrations have made this relationship a central priority.

Yet with a few notable exceptions, progress has fallen short of expectations. Even great breakthroughs in defense ties or the civilian nuclear deal have been accompanied by serious obstacles to real, measurable progress in terms of deals signed, projects launched, and joint activities undertaken. We have extremely deep and substantive ties today and are able to consult on a multitude of issues, but most observers of the day-to-day relationship continue to be underwhelmed.

There is broad agreement that U.S. and Indian strategic requirements are in almost complete alignment on major issues including terrorism, the environment, regional stability, and counterproliferation. We agree on the need for an international order based on rules and norms of behavior, secure flows of energy and commerce, and global action to combat climate change. Our goals are most often in sync. The challenges our nations face at home are also surprisingly similar: ensuring the growth of the middle class and good jobs; providing good governance; dealing with violence and discrimination based on race, religion, gender; and securing sustainable energy and water for future generations.

Not surprisingly, however, given our very different history and circumstances, American and Indian approaches to problems—the ways we choose to pursue these often similar ends—frequently differ and sometimes clash. This will remain true under a Modi administration, and leaders in both countries will need to confront this reality if they want to realize the potential of this partnership.

Both the United States and India are coming through difficult periods. Both will do much better if they take this partnership to the next level. The diplomatic infrastructure exists to make substantial progress: we have a robust and broad Strategic Dialogue and a well-established set of bilateral defense forums. We see good signs of commitment from both sides with the early scheduling of a Strategic Dialogue in New Delhi and with rapid steps to restart the nearly defunct U.S.-India Trade Policy Forum. The early meeting of President Obama and Prime Minister Modi can give these efforts the strategic direction they require.

At the Center for American Progress, we believe this new political phase in India provides an opportunity to make substantial progress in the next 5 years. Next week we are launching a project we call ''India: 2020'' to develop a vision for what our nations can realistically achieve by the end of this decade. Real progress will require high expectations from leaders in both nations and extreme candor about obstacles as well as opportunities.

A WARM WELCOME AND HIGH EXPECTATIONS

Narendra Modi ran on a promise of delivering ''surajya'' or good governance to Indian citizens from all classes, castes, and communities. That is the bar against which he will be judged by the Indian electorate, and it is a promise the United States should welcome and help with wherever possible.

Prime Minister Modi is sending good signals, especially to India's famously complex bureaucracy, with rules against nepotism and steps to improve efficiency. But his to-do list is extraordinarily long and the release of his first budget suggests a careful, step-by-step approach, offering glimpses of what might lie ahead without any radical changes.

Caps on Foreign Direct Investment for the defense insurance sectors were lifted to 49 percent. Defense spending was increased about 12 percent. A commitment to ''smart cities'' and major infrastructure was restated, but resources were not allocated. No major changes were made to entitlements. The FDI cap increases will be welcomed by American business, but they are relatively minor changes that were advocated for by members of the previous government. It will take more than this to get India back to 8 percent growth. So while we should welcome these steps as an opening salvo, we await what future steps Modi will take.

Modi's commitment to good governance is the best way to engage on the difficult and often emotional issues that come with his elevation to power as a strong nationalist with conservative Hindu credentials. He is not likely to let lingering resentment over the denial of his visa in 2005 undermine U.S.-India cooperation in areas that will advance his national priorities. However, the warmth of his welcome in the United States this fall is important. There is no point in taking half measures with the duly elected leader of the world's largest democracy. Congress should invite Prime Minister Modi to address a joint meeting, as was done by his two immediate predecessors, Prime Minister Singh and Prime Minister Vajpayee.

This does not mean being timid about concerns: Prime Minister Modi's commitment to secularism, human rights, and harmony among India's majority and minority communities will ultimately define his legacy and India's continued success and stability. But the United States must take a forward-looking approach. Modi has been cleared by Indian courts of any charges in the 2002 Gujarat riots, which claimed over 1,000 lives and elicited no apology or compensation for victims. Now, as the duly elected leader of the country, he has promised good governance, and that will require him to deliver justice for all Indian communities.

Modi has made positive steps so far in the conduct of international affairs, starting with his invitation of all India's neighbors, including Pakistan, to his inauguration. The United States will be able to engage with Modi on regional issues—not just on stability in Afghanistan and Pakistan, but also on Nepal, Bangladesh, Sri Lanka, and the Maldives. We will be able to work with India on relations with countries from Myanmar to Japan to Australia. Modi is likely to seek a productive dynamic with China, but on the campaign trail he showed that he will be willing to stand up to China by criticizing Beijing's expansionist tendencies.

The potential to work with Modi is very high and crosses every important policy area. Challenges will come if he proves unable or unwilling to make the more difficult reforms that bring India into the global system or if he seeks to over-centralize control. India is a decentralized system, somewhere between the United States and the European Union in the way it functions. The states will demand a significant degree of control over how reforms play out in their own territories.

DEEPENING THE DEFENSE PARTNERSHIP

A decade ago, defense sales were virtually zero. Today, sales have topped $9 billion and defense remains a consistent bright spot in U.S.-India relations. The 2005 New Framework for Defense Cooperation set the stage for this robust defense trade, and U.S. systems like the P–8i to the C130–J have delivered capabilities and reliability that India needs without the scandals and corruption of many other Indian procurements. The U.S. and India have also continued to deepen a very substantial slate of defense exercises, including India's full participation for the first time with 22 other nations in RIMPAC, the world's largest naval exercise underway right now off Hawaii.

The Modi government seems committed to substantial reform of the Indian defense sector, with steps likely to include more flexible offset policies, greater foreign investment as seen in the FDI cap increase, and moves toward breaking up some of the state-run defense sector. These are the kinds of reforms that will make investment in India worthwhile for big international defense companies.

These reforms are also necessary steps for India to be able to take advantage of the various offers pending from the Department of Defense through the Defense Trade and Technology Initiative, or DTTI. Launched by former Secretary Panetta and continued by Secretary Hagel, DTTI offers a breakthrough path to move from sales to high levels of coproduction and codevelopment of future defense systems. The initiative serves to identify possible joint projects of strategic value and streamline and make the U.S. technology transfer and licensing processes more transparent. It has not yet been fully matched by a similar effort on the Indian side, and the U.S. should encourage India to identify its own priorities for codevelopment and to analyze its own bureaucratic constraints on cooperation.

The most exciting offer from the DTTI was for codevelopment of the next generation Javelin antitank missile, an offer the U.S. has made to no other country. India could procure Javelin to meet near term needs and join the U.S. in developing the next generation, which is something the U.S. Army and the Indian Army will both need. The U.S. government worked with industry to identify dozens of possible options for coproduction and codevelopment in everything from helicopters to communications equipment, and an Indian decision to move forward with one or more of these by the time Prime Minister Modi and President Obama meet in September would be a very strong signal that effort put into this partnership can pay off.

Reform of the India's Defense Public Sector will be key to making more of these coproduction and codevelopment deals feasible. U.S. companies will be more interested given the new 49 percent FDI cap, but they will be seeking to make a good business case, and that will be easier with private rather than public sector Indian partners.

There are several short-term steps to take in order to set a positive tone for defense. First, some long-pending sales could be concluded. For example, Chinook and Apache helicopters, as well as M777 Howitzers could be finalized by the time Secretary Hagel visits India later this summer. Second, India and the U.S. could increase their mutual commitment to defense exercises. India was frustrated last year when the U.S. canceled Red Flag air exercises due to the sequester, and the U.S. has been frustrated by India's refusal to include multilateral partners in some U.S.-India exercises. The previous Defense Minister indicated an intention to reduce the overall number of exercises as well. Both nations should commit to a robust set of exercises of increasing complexity and to involving more multilateral partners, including a resumption of Japanese participation in the Malabar naval exercises.

The defense relationship is governed by the 2005 New Framework on Defense Cooperation, which established a strategic partnership in defense and paved the way for remarkable progress. The New Framework created several regular forums to meet and discuss key issues, all reporting to the annual Defense Policy Group. The 2005 agreement was drafted for a 10-year term, and the time is now for the U.S. and India to take stock of that agreement and set forth a new vision to run through 2025. This should be a rigorous reappraisal, looking at both successes as well as where the framework came up short. It should ideally be reviewed as part of an effort led from the White House to rationalize the entire slate of U.S.-India cooperative forums.

ECONOMIC LIBERALIZATION AND TIES OF COMMERCE, ENERGY, AND BUSINESS

India was unprepared when financial turmoil struck. As growth stagnated, the previous coalition government was unable to drive through additional liberalization and resorted to short-sighted and damaging moves like retroactive taxation and curbs on capital outflows. Coupled with the continued inability to address major obstacles on trade and investment like Intellectual Property Rights, or IPR, protection and excessive local content requirements, these steps seemed to put economic liberalization in a deep freeze and drove away investment.

India ranks 139th on the World Bank's Doing Business Index, and Modi's reforms will improve that rating if they can make India more appealing to international business. The BJP campaigned on a commitment to jump-start reform. The current budget is incremental with modest improvements in FDI caps and few changes from the interim budget of the prior government. Former Finance Minister Chidambaram went so far as to claim credit for the BJP budget as a continuation of his policies. This may have disappointed business, but it could give the Indian Government much-needed time to explain to the public what specific reforms it plans to under- take and how they will help the nation.

Finance Minister Arun Jaitley tried to calm international business leaders still smarting under the retroactive taxation on companies like Vodafone, but he didn't undo the taxation, saying instead, ''The sovereign right of the Government to under-take retrospective legislation is unquestionable. However, this power has to be exercised with extreme caution and judiciousness keeping in mind the impact of each such measure on the economy and the overall investment climate. This Government will not ordinarily bring about any change retrospectively which creates a fresh liability.''

Jaitley's statement provides cold comfort to multinational firms who have been hoping for something more like what they heard in the campaign when Modi called retroactive taxation a ''breach of trust'' that could drive away investment. The new Indian Government also looks poised to block the World Trade Organization trade facilitation agreement reached in Bali last December over concerns about the impact on India's food security program. The deadline is July 31. This could make India the cause of failure for the first significant WTO accomplishment in years.

The United States and India have some options on trade. The best remains conclusion of a bilateral investment treaty, or BIT, but the negotiations have been mired since they started 5 years ago. U.S. Trade Representative Mike Froman has made the right gestures by planning to restart the U.S.-India Trade Policy Forum while holding firm on IPR and local content issues. The distance between the two sides on a BIT, especially with regard to a dispute resolution mechanism, could remain too great to bridge in the near term. Intensified negotiations with the new government are the only way to proceed, perhaps with a new and realistic target date for completion. It's also worth introducing India to the idea of eventually joining a future Trans-Pacific Partnership, should that process prove successful.

ENERGY AND CLIMATE

India faces significant and intertwined energy security, energy poverty, and climate challenges. It is currently on track to become the world's largest coal importer in about a decade, and Prime Minister Modi aims to provide basic access to power and water for every Indian house in less than 10 years—an important and large task given that 300 million Indians currently lack electricity. India is also one of the world's largest greenhouse gas emitters, and is highly vulnerable to the impacts of climate change.

With the United States simultaneously grappling with its own energy and climate challenges, there are untapped opportunities for mutually beneficial cooperation. Since 2010, CAP has cochaired a Track II dialogue on climate change and clean energy with India comprised of high-level former government officials, thought leaders, and influential individuals from the NGO and business communities. With annual meetings in Delhi and Washington, DC, the Track II has provided a forum for the exchange of new and innovative ideas, as well as produced insights that have helped to shape government policy and define new areas for enhanced bilateral cooperation. At its most recent meeting in February, it recommended:

Enhancing cooperation on clean energy development: To enable the rapid growth of renewable energy, the U.S. and India should continue expanding their R&D collaboration, while also building capacity in science, engineering, and other business models to spur technological innovation and entrepreneurship in the field. It also should do so by avoiding trade disputes in the renewable sector. Both countries have immense opportunities for growth in renewable energy, yet we find ourselves locked in WTO disputes with one another over local source requirement, subsidies, and tariffs surrounding solar power. The two sides should seek to develop a set of principles to avoid future WTO filings. They should aim for prior consultation on national policy requirements, identify bilateral dispute resolution methods, and exercise restraint in filing disputes that affect renewable energy. Resolving the current solar dispute in ways that meet the aims of both nations will open the door to substantial cooperation on large solar projects.

Reducing Hydrofluorocarbons: The U.S. and India have the opportunity to advance global action on phasing down hydrofluorocarbons, a short-lived but highly potent greenhouse gas. The U.S. and India can lead the pursuit of a global agreement on HFCs by pushing for technology-agnostic global standards to curb HFCs and ensure energy efficiency performance so that new technologies do not increase other greenhouse gas emissions.

Building Climate Resilience: In addition to lowering emissions, the U.S. and India will need to ensure community resilience against climate impacts including sea-level rise, more frequent flooding, and extreme weather. Hurricane Sandy demonstrated how damaging intense storms can be, even in a prepared city. We need much more research on the most effective ways to respond to climate change. Urban and coastal resilience are two key areas for the U.S. and India to pursue joint research and pilot projects. The research partnership could be modeled on the existing U.S.-India Joint Clean Energy Research and Development Center.

India is exploring other energy options that would reduce its coal dependence and expand energy access, such as through increased use of natural gas and nuclear power in its electricity mix. It is in the United States interest to engage India on the safe and responsible development and use of such fuels. This would include discussions about the safe development, transmission and use of natural gas. Engagement should also include discussion of the political and legal issues that surround development of nuclear power generation projects in India. They are difficult and complicated, but should be grappled with.

INDIA'S ROLE IN THE REGION AND ASIA-PACIFIC

For the past decade, the United States has played a critical role in welcoming India's rise as a global power. The Bush administration drove international acceptance of India as a responsible nuclear power outside the confines of the Non-Proliferation Treaty. It is easy to forget how controversial and politically difficult that was. The Obama administration welcomed India as a partner, with public calls for India to gain a permanent seat on the U.N. Security Council. And the United States has supported Indian membership in global nonproliferation regimes and treats India as an adherent so long as it keeps its export controls in conformity with the regimes. In many ways the United States has embraced a form of Indian exceptionalism because it calculates that India will work to advance mutual interests. That is a good bet, and India is rising to the challenge of global and regional leadership.

India is the anchor of the most strategically vital region on earth, stretching from the Persian Gulf and spanning northeast to Japan and southeast to Australia. The challenges across this region are growing and the United States and India should look to one another for ideas and leadership from the Middle East to Central Asia to East Asia. India will be deeply impacted by developments in the Middle East given its dependence on energy flows and large expatriate communities. It will play a critical role in the long-term stability and connectivity for Afghanistan and Central Asia. It is leading efforts to build eastward connectivity given the new potential of a reforming Myanmar, and it is managing, what should now be termed major power relations of its own with Japan and China.

The United States decision to treat India as a major power can continue to encourage India to take a greater role. The United States has important stake and conviction in maintaining free and safe trade lines and waterways throughout the Pacific, and while India has traditionally remained hesitant to active participation in maintaining regional security, it supports unimpeded rights of passage and maritime rights in accordance with international law. For example, India offers naval support to the counter piracy mission in the Gulf of Aden while refusing to join the multinational task force there.

Seventy years ago, India's first Prime Minister Jawaharlal Nehru stated, "The Pacific is likely to take the place of the Atlantic in the future as the nerve center of the world [and] though not directly a Pacific state, India will inevitably exercise an important influence there . . . [and] is the pivot around which these problems will have to be considered.'' Nehru's words have proven true, and India is seeking a greater leadership role in the rest of Asia. It is welcomed by ASEAN nations and the United States. Total India-ASEAN trade increased by 37 percent in 2011–2012 to reach USD79.3 billion and the total U.S.-ASEAN goods trade increased by 60 percent in the past decade, peaking at USD206 billion in 2013. The United States and India have a shared interest in collaborating to ensure global standards and international norms and should look instinctively to each other to mitigate territorial disputes and transnational threats that arise throughout this stretch.

India's eastern and western neighbors provide great economic opportunity and partnership within its own region. Managing these relationships will be a crucial challenge that will necessitate paramount energy and diplomacy. There have been positive signs from Pakistan and India's new governments to seize this opportunity to build toward trade normalization and regional security, and there are high hopes that this remains a positive upward trajectory.

The complexities of South Asia's transnational problems, such as refugee crises stemming from ethnic violence to climate-related migration, defy national solutions. There is urgency for India and its neighbors to build cooperative relationship and promote a regional framework that incorporates the perspectives of all nations involved.

CONCLUSION

Mr. Chairman and members of the committee, let me close by saying that the U.S.-India bilateral relationship has quietly and steadily grown under the leadership of like-minded individuals across party lines in both countries. There remain gaps between what our two nations are doing and what our two nations are capable of doing. However, I do agree with President Obama that the U.S.-India relationship will be one of the defining partnerships of the 21st century. This partnership will need continued engagement and nurturing and it's a commitment that would reap mutual benefits.

Senator KAINE. Thank you, Mr. Singh.
Ms. Curtis.

STATEMENT OF LISA CURTIS, SENIOR RESEARCH FELLOW, THE HERITAGE FOUNDATION, WASHINGTON, DC

Ms. CURTIS. Thank you, Chairman Kaine, for inviting me here today. It is an honor.

The BJP's victory and assumption of power provides an opportunity to build the United States-India relationship. I think it bodes well for the country's economic prospects as well as its role in global affairs more generally. The previous Manmohan Singh government had been weakened by a series of corruption scandals. It was distracted by governance problems, which led to the stagnation of the relationship. Of course, you mentioned how ties were further strained by the Devyani Khobragade episode.

So now we have an opportunity to move beyond that phase in the relationship and reinvigorate ties on a variety of fronts, whether it be defense, security, economic cooperation, counterterrorism, or other issues of mutual concern. We have heard a lot about how Prime Minister Modi is expected to revive the Indian economy and encourage private sector growth. His track record in making Gujarat one of the most investor-friendly states gives confidence that he will implement policy changes that will help revive the economy.

Regarding foreign policy, the Modi-led government is expected to pursue a more robust and assertive approach and enhance India's influence and prestige on the global stage. While a more assertive approach to foreign policy could pose some challenges to the United States, I think by and large it will open up opportunities for the United States to draw closer to India with regard to defense and security issues.

With regard specifically to China, the Modi government is likely to pursue a multifaceted approach which involves both simultaneously improving trade and investment ties while also focusing on building up its own strategic and military capabilities to guard against the possibility of Chinese aggression along their disputed borders.

The BJP election manifesto did not mention China specifically. However, it did commit to a massive infrastructure development program along the Line of Actual Control, which is the disputed border between India and China in the states of Arunachal Pradesh and Sikkim. Modi's call a few months ago for China to abandon its expansionist attitude shows that the Modi government is wary of Chinese territorial ambitions, especially in light of last April's border incident in which Chinese troops camped for 3 weeks several miles inside Indian territory in the Ladakh region of Kashmir.

The Modi government has been receptive to Chinese wooing over the last 6 weeks, including an early visit by the Chinese Foreign Minister to New Delhi just 3 weeks after Modi had assumed office and Monday's meeting between Modi and the Chinese President on the fringes of the BRIC summit.

Prime Minister Modi has also demonstrated interest in setting a positive tone in relations with Islamabad by inviting Prime Minister Nawaz Sharif to his swearing-in ceremony, but still a major terrorist attack inside India with links to Pakistan could quickly reverse this positive momentum. And having criticized Prime Minister Singh for being too soft on Pakistan, Modi would be under pressure to react strongly in the face of any new terrorist provocation.

Moreover, there is growing concern about the impact on Indo-Pakistani relations of the United States drawdown from Afghanistan and whether this could in fact re-ignite the Kashmir conflict.

So what initiatives can the United States pursue with the new Indian Government to take advantage of this opportunity to bolster the relationship? First is in the realm of cooperation in the Asia-Pacific. Now, Indian officials were initially cautious in their response to the U.S. policy of rebalancing toward the Asia-Pacific. But I think the Chinese border provocation of April 2013 may prompt New Delhi to become more open to this idea of a robust United States role in the region.

You talked about trilateral cooperation. I think there is a real opportunity to build United States-India-Japan trilateral cooperation.

Prime Minister Abe of Japan and Prime Minister Modi have a personal relationship. Modi has visited Japan. So I think there is a real opportunity to bolster that trilateral dialogue.

I would just mention that the Heritage Foundation conducted a track two quadrilateral dialogue with an Indian think tank, a Japanese think tank, and an Australian think tank in December. I think it is important—even though the stage is not set for a formal quadrilateral dialogue, I think it is useful to have these track two dialogues so that, in the event where there might be a need to start an official quadrilateral dialogue, we can put that into place.

Second is defense. As mentioned, the United States and India need to renew the 10-year defense framework agreement and build on the defense, trade, and technology initiative that was launched in 2012. Regarding civil nuclear cooperation, I think there is an opportunity to make a fresh push on changing the liability issue. While in opposition, the BJP certainly opposed the nuclear deal and pushed for this liability legislation that has complicated United States companies' ability to get involved in the civil nuclear sector in India. However, now that the BJP is in power, I think there may be a willingness to soften their position and build a political consensus around resolution of this issue.

Fourth, nonproliferation. The United States should be pressing for India's membership in the major multilateral nonproliferation groupings, such as the Nuclear Suppliers Group, the Missile Technology Control Regime, and other groupings. This is something that the United States should be pushing for in the future. This is important to bring India into these groupings rather than have it be outside of this process. That is good for global stability.

Fifth, Afghanistan and counterterrorism. We need to deepen this dialogue and certainly Afghanistan needs to be part of the counterterrorism dialogue and we need to increase our consultations.

Lastly, I just want to flag very quickly the remote possibility that the religious freedom issue could become an irritant in United States-India relations. I think Modi has definitely distanced himself from communal politics during the election campaign and he focused instead on the economy and good governance. However, religious minorities in India remain concerned that the BJP could pursue a communal agenda that would be detrimental to their interests. So this is just something that we have to keep an eye on.

So in conclusion, the election of the BJP government is likely to have a positive impact on the Indian economy and reestablish confidence in India as a global power. If the United States demonstrates its willingness to establish closer ties with the new government, the BJP is likely to reciprocate and we could both focus on achieving that vision of a durable and strategic partnership.

Thank you.

[The prepared statement of Ms. Curtis follows:]

PREPARED STATEMENT OF LISA CURTIS

My name is Lisa Curtis. I am Senior Research Fellow on South Asia in the Asian Studies Center at The Heritage Foundation. The views I express in this testimony are my own, and should not be construed as representing any official position of The Heritage Foundation.[1]

The Bharatiya Janata Party's (BJP) landslide victory in India's recent parliamentary elections bodes well for the country's future economic prospects, as well as for its role in global affairs, including relations with the U.S. Having won 282 parliamentary seats, the BJP surprised even its own party members by becoming the first Indian party in 30 years to win a majority of seats on its own. This means that the BJP will not have to rely on coalition partners to remain in power, being, instead, in a relatively strong position to implement policies, including economic reforms and other measures that could help restore investor confidence and improve India's GDP growth rate.

The new government led by Prime Minister Narendra Modi is expected to pursue a more robust foreign policy than its Congress Party predecessor, and to enhance India's influence and prestige on the global stage. While a more assertive approach to foreign policy than was pursued under the second Manmohan Singh government could pose some challenges to U.S. policymakers, it also will open opportunities for the U.S. to draw closer to India. New Delhi and Washington share similar strategic objectives, whether they involve countering terrorism, maintaining open and free seaways, or hedging against China's rise.

OPPORTUNITY TO REINVIGORATE U.S.–INDIAN RELATIONSHIP

The election of the BJP is welcome news for the beleaguered Indian economy. Prime Minister Modi was voted into power on promises to revive Indian economic growth, rein in corruption, and create jobs for the rapidly growing youth population. India's GDP growth rate has recently dipped below 5 percent, down from around 8 percent 2 years ago.

Foreign investors have been optimistic that Modi's election would help turn the economy around. Modi's track record of making Gujarat one of India's most investor friendly states when he served as its chief minister has sparked confidence that Modi will prioritize reviving the economy and encouraging private-sector growth. Some of this optimism was tempered following the introduction of the Indian budget last week, however. The budget, presented to the Parliament by Finance Minister Arun Jaitley on July 10, did not go as far in opening up the economy, adjusting fiscal imbalances, and cutting subsidies as international investors had expected, and markets reacted tepidly to the budget announcement.

One of the main reasons why the U.S.-India relationship has foundered over the last few years, is that the previous Singh government was unwilling to enact necessary economic reforms. The Singh government also had been weakened by a series of corruption scandals and was distracted from building ties with the U.S. by domestic governance challenges during most of its second term.

Indo-U.S. ties were further strained in December 2013 when the U.S. arrested Indian diplomat Devyani Khobragade for underpaying her Indian maid while serving at the Indian consulate in New York. The details of Khobragade's arrest, particularly reports that she was handcuffed in front of her children's school and strip-searched while in detention, infuriated the Indian public.[2] Washington, for its part, was taken aback by the fierce Indian reaction, which included withdrawing diplomatic privileges for U.S. diplomats and removing security barriers at the U.S. Embassy in New Delhi.

The BJP's assumption of power offers an opportunity to move beyond the Khobragade episode and revive ties by focusing on building cooperation on defense, security, economic and trade, counterterrorism, and other issues of mutual concern. The previous BJP-led government (1998–2004) was instrumental in elevating ties between Washington and New Delhi and in laying a solid foundation for a strategic partnership.

ROBUST FOREIGN POLICY

The new Modi government is expected to pursue a more robust foreign policy than its Congress Party predecessor, and to enhance India's influence and prestige on the global stage. The BJP election manifesto states that the BJP "believes a resurgent India must get its rightful place in the comity of nations and international institutions. The vision is to fundamentally reboot and reorient the foreign policy goals . . . so that it leads to an economically stronger India, and its voice is heard in the international fora."[3] A greater Indian willingness to acknowledge external threats and take initiatives to mitigate those threats could result in increased U.S.-Indian cooperation on a variety of defense, security, nuclear, and maritime issues.

China

The new BJP government is likely to adopt a multifaceted policy toward China, entailing both greater economic engagement with Beijing and a willingness to stand up to any perceived Chinese aggression along disputed borders. At the same time,

India will focus on building up its military and strategic capabilities in an effort to keep pace with Chinese military modernization.

Sino-Indian trade dipped slightly in 2013 to $66 billion (from $74 billion in 2012), but China remains India's biggest trading partner. While the BJP is likely to pursue closer economic ties with China, in February, Modi called on China to "abandon its expansionist attitude." A major event that will shape the new government's policy-making toward Beijing is the April 2013 border incident in which Chinese troops camped for 3 weeks several miles inside Indian territory in the Ladakh region of the state of Jammu and Kashmir. The incursion—probably the most serious by the Chinese in over two decades—has convinced Indian strategists that it must increasingly factor the potential threat of conflict over its disputed borders with China into its security planning and projections.

Signs of India's and China's deep-seated border disagreements have been surfacing over the last several years, and it is likely that such friction will continue, given the unsettled borders, China's interest in consolidating its hold on Tibet, and India's expanding influence in Asia. In recent years, China has increasingly pressured India over the disputed borders by questioning Indian sovereignty over Arunachal Pradesh; stepping up probing operations along different parts of the shared frontier; and building up its military infrastructure, as well as expanding its network of road, rail, and air links, in the border areas. India accuses China of illegally occupying more than 14,000 square miles of its territory on its northern border in Kashmir, while China lays claim to more than 34,000 square miles of India's northeastern state of Arunachal Pradesh. India is a long-term host to the Dalai Lama and about 100,000 Tibetan refugees, although the Indian Government forbids them from participating in any political activity.

The BJP manifesto does not mention China specifically, but it commits to a "special emphasis on massive infrastructure development, especially along the Line of Actual Control [the disputed border between India and China] in Arunachal Pradesh and Sikkim." [4] Developing the areas along the disputed border allows India to strengthen its territorial claims and defend itself against any potential Chinese aggression.

The Modi government has welcomed Chinese overtures, such as the early visit by Chinese Foreign Minister Wang Yi to New Delhi just 3 weeks after Modi assumed office, and a bilateral meeting between Modi and Chinese President Xi Jinping on Monday on the fringes of the Brazil, Russia, India, China, and South Africa (BRICS) summit in Brazil. It is unclear why Modi postponed a trip to Tokyo scheduled for early July, but the optics of Modi engaging two senior Chinese leaders before holding any meetings with Japanese officials demonstrates New Delhi's interest in building positive momentum with Beijing.

The BJP leadership likely wants to avoid any early controversies in the India-China relationship like it experienced during its previous tenure when the BJP-led government cited the "Chinese threat" as justification for its nuclear tests in May 1998. One year later, however, New Delhi was pleasantly surprised by Beijing's neutral position on the Indo-Pakistani Kargil crisis, a position that helped spur a thaw in Sino-Indian relations. Then-Prime Minister Atal Bihari Vajpayee made a historic visit to Beijing in July 2003, during which each side appointed a "special representative" to upgrade and regularize their border discussions.

Japan

In the past few years, India has focused increasingly on buttressing security ties with Japan, South Korea, and Vietnam to meet the challenges of a rapidly rising China. Indo-Japanese ties, in particular, are expected to get a major boost under Modi's administration since Modi and Japanese Prime Minister Shinzo Abe are both increasingly concerned about China and appear prepared to take new policy directions to deal with the challenges posed by Beijing's rapid military and economic ascendance. They have also developed a close personal rapport. As chief minister, Modi traveled to Japan in 2007, marking the first time an Indian chief minister had traveled to the country. Modi was one of the first foreign dignitaries to congratulate Abe when he was reelected in 2012.[5] The recent postponement of Modi's visit to Japan is all the more perplexing, given the history of the personal relationship between Abe and Modi.

For his part, Abe has been a longtime supporter of stronger ties between India and Japan, and initiated the idea of the Quad (the U.S.-Australia-Japan-India security grouping) during his previous tenure in 2006. Abe was also one of the first leaders to acknowledge that the Pacific and Indian Oceans should be linked strategically on the basis of the need to preserve free and open seaways, thus helping to coin the term "Indo-Pacific." [6]

While their economic ties pale in comparison to those between China and India, Indo-Japanese diplomatic engagement has intensified in recent years. Japanese Emperor Akihito paid a rare visit to New Delhi in late 2013. Indian Prime Minister Singh made a historic 4-day visit to Tokyo in May 2013, in which the two sides signed a joint statement pledging nuclear cooperation and expanded joint naval exercises. Japan also endorsed India for membership in the multilateral export control regimes, signaling Tokyo's acceptance of India's nuclear status.

Russia

India and Russia are likely to maintain their historically close partnership under the new Indian Government. Russia remains India's top defense supplier, providing about 70 percent of India's defense requirements. The uncertainty surrounding the withdrawal of U.S. and NATO forces from Afghanistan has brought New Delhi and Moscow even closer in their shared goal to prevent a Pakistan-supported Taliban from regaining power in Kabul.

Differences in policies toward Russia could become a major irritant in India-U.S. relations, particularly if Russian President Vladimir Putin further extends Russian claims on Ukraine, and New Delhi continues to provide unqualified support for Putin. India tacitly supported President Putin's annexation of the Crimea on March 18, 2014, by acknowledging Russia's "legitimate interests" there and deciding not to back U.S. and EU sanctions against Russia.

Pakistan

Modi has demonstrated interest in setting a positive tone in relations with Islamabad by inviting Pakistani Prime Minister Nawaz Sharif to his swearing-in ceremony, an unprecedented move by an Indian leader. Still, a major terrorist attack in India with links to Pakistan could quickly reverse the current positive trajectory in Indo-Pakistani relations. Former Prime Minister Singh had shown a great deal of forbearance toward Pakistan, and a personal commitment to maintaining peaceful ties with Islamabad, even following attacks in India that were traced back to Pakistan-based groups. Having criticized Singh for being too soft on Pakistan, Modi would be under pressure to react strongly in the face of a terrorist provocation.

Moreover, there is growing concern about the impact on Indo-Pakistani relations of the international troop drawdown in Afghanistan and whether the Kashmir conflict could reignite. According to Indian officials, there was an increase in militant infiltration from Pakistani territory into Indian-held Kashmir in 2013. Last August, Indo-Pakistani military tensions escalated for a brief period when a series of incidents along the Line of Control (LoC) that divides Kashmir led to the killing of five Indian soldiers and a Pakistani civilian. The incidents led to charged rhetoric on both sides and dashed hopes for a potential meeting of the Indian and Pakistani leaders on the fringes of the 2013 U.N. General Assembly.

Modi is attempting to strike a balance between sounding a tough message on terrorism, while leaving the door open for improved Indo-Pakistani economic relations. In an interview with The Times of India in early May, Modi said that both countries faced the common enemy of widespread poverty and that he would be ready to "write a new chapter" in relations if Pakistan demonstrates that it is committed to stopping terrorist attacks from being launched from its territory.[7]

When Indo-Pakistani tensions have escalated in the past, such as during the 2001–2002 military standoff and in the aftermath of the 2008 Mumbai attacks, the U.S. played a key behind-the-scenes role in walking both countries back from the brink of conflict. But the U.S. inability to convince Pakistan to cut support to anti-Indian militants over the last several years may lead the new Indian Government to conclude that it cannot rely on the U.S. to help de-escalate a potential future crisis with Islamabad, and instead must address the threat from Pakistan on its own.

DEFENSE TRADE AND COOPERATION

The U.S. should continue to position itself to help India fulfill its defense modernization requirements and enable American companies to pursue partnerships that support India's interest in developing its domestic defense production sector. The BJP's election manifesto highlighted the need to modernize India's Armed Forces and increase research and development in the defense sector, with the goal of developing indigenous defense technologies and "fast-tracking" defense purchases.[8] The budget that was released in India last week raised total defense spending by 12 percent to $38 billion for the Indian fiscal year ending in March 2015.[9] It also raised foreign direct investment caps in the defense sector to 49 percent, up from the current limit of 26 percent, but still short of what many defense investors had expected. India's Department of Industrial Policy and Promotion (DIPP) had recommended in May that the government make more drastic changes with regard to FDI in the defense sector. The DIPP proposed allowing 49 percent FDI in defense projects where no technology transfer was involved; 74 percent in cases of technology transfer; and 100 percent for manufacturing state-of-the-art equipment.[10]

The U.S.-India Defense Trade and Technology Initiative (DTTI), launched in 2012, is aimed at breaking down barriers between the two countries' defense bureaucracies and enhancing defense trade and technology exchange. India is expected to spend over $100 billion on defense equipment over the next 8 years. In 2013, U.S. military exports to India totaled $1.9 billion with delivery of C–17 heavy transport aircraft and P–81 long-range maritime reconnaissance and antisubmarine warfare planes. The U.S. has signed over $13 billion in total defense contracts with India over the past several years, but still lags behind Russia as a defense supplier to India.

Maritime Issues

India has the world's fifth-largest Navy and Asia's only operational aircraft carrier.[11] In its manifesto, the BJP made special mention of the need to refurbish India's navy. A series of mishaps on Indian submarines and ships over the past year have raised questions about India's ability to achieve its naval ambitions. The most serious problems have occurred with its Russian Kilo-class submarines. There was an explosion on the INS (Indian Naval Submarine) Sindhurakshak in August 2013 that killed 18 officers and sailors, and a fire on the INS Sindhuratna in February, which led to the resignation of the naval chief.[12]

Nuclear Issues

The previous BJP-led government, under Atal Bihari Vajpayee, surprised the world and invoked sanctions when it tested nuclear weapons shortly after assuming office in May 1998. The bold action says something about the BJP's willingness to assert India's national security interests, but the decision must also be viewed in context. Former Congress Party Prime Minister, Narasima Rao, was close to conducting nuclear tests in 1995, until the U.S. Government preempted the test by delivering a demarche to the Rao government based on intelligence it had collected on Indian test preparations. The 1998 decision to test also was related to negotiations surrounding the Comprehensive Test Ban Treaty (CTBT) and India's interest in ensuring that it tested its nuclear weapons before the CTBT came into force.[13]

POTENTIAL STUMBLING BLOCK: COMMUNAL AGENDA

When U.S. President Barack Obama called Prime Minister Modi shortly after the election results were announced to congratulate him on his victory and to invite him to Washington, he sent a signal that the U.S. is ready to do business with Modi and move beyond the issue of the 2002 Gujarat riots.

The U.S. had revoked Modi's tourist visa in 2005 under the terms of its International Religious Freedom Act for failing to halt Hindu-Muslim riots in 2002 that killed more than 1,000 people—mainly Muslims—over the course of 3 days in the state of Gujarat. The riots followed an incident in which a group of Muslims set fire to a train carrying Hindu pilgrims destined for Ahmedabad and passing through the town of Godhra. Modi, who was Gujarat's chief minister at the time, allowed funeral processions in the streets of Ahmedabad the next day, and the state government failed to control Hindu mobs that went on a systematic rampage murdering Muslims. Modi was accused of turning a blind eye to the violence, or worse, although the Indian courts have cleared him of criminal activity.

U.S. officials should give Modi a chance to prove he will not be a divisive leader and will work instead to improve the Indian economy for everyone's benefit. Modi stayed away from communal politics during the election campaign and focused instead on the economy and good governance. In his first speech to the Indian Parliament on June 11, he acknowledged that India's Muslims lagged behind the rest of the nation in socioeconomic terms and noted the importance of addressing this challenge, saying: "If one organ of the body remains weak, the body cannot be termed as healthy . . . We are committed to this . . . We don't see it as appeasement."

In the past, the BJP has supported policy positions considered divisive by the Muslim minority community. These include support for the construction of a Hindu temple at Ayodhya, where a mosque was destroyed by Hindus in 1992; the establishment of a uniform civil code, rather than allowing Muslims to maintain certain personal laws based on religious custom; and repeal of Article 370 of the Indian Constitution, which provides the state of Jammu and Kashmir special autonomous status. The BJP did not pursue these controversial issues when it held power previously (1998–2004), mainly because it lacked support from its coalition partners. Even though the BJP now holds a majority on its own, Modi will have to consider the costs of prioritizing a "hindutva" (Hindu religious and cultural nationalism) agenda in terms of political support at home and abroad, and the possibility that doing so could undermine his goals of building a strong and prosperous India with a positive global image.

Christians, numbering about 25 million in India, have also faced harassment and violent attacks by organizations following a hindutva agenda. Christians feel especially vulnerable in states that have adopted anticonversion laws. The anticonversion laws are aimed at preventing "forced conversion" but have been misused by Hindu zealots to harass Christians and to legitimize mob violence.

It remains to be seen to what degree the BJP might focus on trying to rebuild the Ram Temple. Hindus would like access to Ayodhya, as they believe it to be the birthplace of the Hindu god Rama, where a prominent Hindu temple (the Ram Temple) once existed. In 1992, BJP leader L. K. Advani led a protest march to the Babri mosque at Ayodhya that resulted in its destruction by Hindu zealots and ensuing communal riots that killed nearly 2,000. In September 2010, a high court in India ruled that the land at Ayodhya be divided into three segments: one-third for the reconstruction of the Ram Temple; one-third for the Islamic Sunni Waqf Board; and one-third for another Hindu group. The 2014 BJP manifesto expresses support for rebuilding the Ram Temple within the confines of the Indian constitution.

U.S. POLICY RECOMMENDATIONS

The rise to power of the BJP, led by now-Prime Minister Modi, creates an opportunity to end the malaise that has taken over India-U.S. relations in the last few years. Modi's upcoming visit to Washington on September 30 is an opportunity for the U.S. administration to demonstrate its commitment to moving relations forward with the new government. U.S. policymakers should consider initiatives in the following areas.

The Asia–Pacific

While Indian strategists assess Pakistan as posing the most immediate threat to India, they increasingly view China as the more important long-term strategic threat. Indian officials were initially cautious in their response to the U.S. policy of rebalancing toward the Asia-Pacific, but the Chinese border provocation in April 2013 may prompt New Delhi to become more open to the idea of a robust U.S. role in the region. A BJP government also will not be constrained or influenced by leftist-leaning politicians who have a knee-jerk aversion to strategic cooperation with the U.S., as was the case with the Congress Party-led government. BJP leaders will continue to resist any policy construed as "containment" of China, however. Modi's strong equation with Japanese Prime Minister Abe also could open opportunities for greater trilateral cooperation among the U.S., India, and Japan, although it is unclear why Modi postponed a trip to Tokyo scheduled for July 3.

Defense

India and the U.S. should renew the 10-year defense framework agreement they signed in 2005 and build on the progress of the Defense Trade and Technology Initiative. Indian willingness to adhere to U.S. technology protection agreements will be critical to moving the Indo-U.S. defense relationship forward.

Civil Nuclear Cooperation

The U.S. should make a fresh push to resolve the nuclear liability issue. While in opposition, the BJP opposed the civil nuclear deal and pushed for nuclear liability legislation that complicated U.S. companies' ability to invest in civil nuclear projects in India. Now that the BJP is in power, the party leaders may be willing to soften their position and build a political consensus around a resolution to the liability issue that would allow U.S. firms to invest in the civil nuclear sector.

Nonproliferation

The U.S. should continue to press for India's membership in the four major multilateral nonproliferation groupings: the Nuclear Suppliers Group (NSG); the Missile Technology Control Regime (MTCR); the Australia Group (which seeks to control the export of chemical and biological weapons); and the Wassenaar Arrangement (which seeks to control the export of conventional arms and dual-use goods). The U.S. and U.K. support India's admission to the NSG, but some NSG members have expressed concern that admitting India will erode the credibility of the Nuclear Nonproliferation Treaty (NPT), since India is not a signatory of the treaty. India should continue to improve its export control processes and the transparency of its strategic nuclear programs to help bolster its case for full membership in the multilateral nonproliferation groupings. The U.S. and other international partners need to develop fresh thinking about India's relationship to the NPT and nonproliferation system that takes into account the reality that India will not join the NPT as a non-weapons state. Though the NSG is closely associated with the NPT, it is also fact that the NSG was originally created in a way that France could join even though it had not yet signed the NPT.[14]

Afghanistan/Counterterrorism

The U.S. should expand and deepen its counterterrorism dialogue and cooperation with India. The future of Afghanistan should be a key component of the Indo-U.S. counterterrorism dialogue, particularly given the alarming situation in Iraq, where Islamist extremists are making gains in the absence of a U.S. force presence in the country. The U.S. should encourage India's economic and political involvement in Afghanistan, which helps bolster the Afghan Government's efforts to fight terrorism. To kick-start the effort, the U.S. should send a high-level multiagency delegation (from the CIA, the Department of Homeland Security, and the National Counterterrorism Center) to India to exchange views on regional terrorist threats.

Indo-Pakistani Relations

U.S. policymakers can take steps to reduce the possibility of deteriorating Indo-Pakistani relations. While U.S. officials should not seek a mediation role, they can work behind the scenes to encourage Indo-Pakistani dialogue and inject ideas for moving a peace process forward. Moreover, the U.S. must maintain pressure on Pakistan to crack down on Kashmir-focused terrorist groups. The Mumbai terrorist attacks of 2008 should be viewed as the culmination of U.S. failure to connect the dots between Pakistani support for Kashmir-focused terrorist groups and the broader international terrorist threat. Washington should also remain vigilant in monitoring the human rights situation inside Jammu and Kashmir, raising concerns with the Indian Government when necessary. In the summer of 2010 protests that turned violent in Kashmir led to the killing of 126 Muslim youth by Indian security forces. The U.S. should encourage trade, joint economic projects, and civil society engagement among the people from both sides of Kashmir.

Religious Freedom

While the new Indian Government is in its early days, so far there is reason for cautious optimism that it will focus on implementing policies beneficial for the Indian economy and that enhance India's international role. Still, the U.S. should engage India on religious freedom issues to ensure that Modi follows through on his promises to meet the needs of all Indian citizens and stays away from controversial policies supported by hardliners within his party and associated organizations.

CONCLUSION

The election of a BJP government is likely to have a positive impact on the Indian economy and reestablish international confidence in India as a global power. If the U.S. demonstrates its willingness to establish close ties with the new government, it is likely that the BJP will reciprocate and the two sides can refocus on achieving the vision of a durable and strategic partnership.

End Notes

[1] The Heritage Foundation is a public policy, research, and educational organization recognized as exempt under section 501(c)(3) of the Internal Revenue Code. It is privately supported and receives no funds from any government at any level, nor does it perform any government or other contract work.

The Heritage Foundation is the most broadly supported think tank in the United States. During 2012, it had nearly 700,000 individual, foundation, and corporate supporters representing every state in the U.S. Its 2012 income came from the following sources: Individuals 81%; Foundations 14%; Corporations 5%.

The top five corporate givers provided The Heritage Foundation with 2 percent of its 2012 income. The Heritage Foundation's books are audited annually by the national accounting firm of McGladrey & Pullen. A list of major donors is available from The Heritage Foundation upon request.

Members of The Heritage Foundation staff testify as individuals discussing their own independent research. The views expressed are their own and do not reflect an institutional position for The Heritage Foundation or its board of trustees.

[2] Annie Gowan and Anne Gearan, ''U.S. Attorney Says Indian Diplomat Arrested 'in the Most Discreet Way Possible,' '' The Washington Post, December 18, 2013.

[3] BJP Election Manifesto 2014.

[4] Ibid.

[5] Palash Ghosh, ''India 2014 Elections: BJP Leader Narendra Modi's Bromance with Japan's Shinzo Abe,'' International Business Times, March 10, 2014.

48

[6] Ambassador Karl F. Inderfurth and Ted Osius, "India's 'Look East' and America's 'Asia Pivot': Converging Interests," U.S.-India Insight, Vol. 3, No. 3 (March 2013).
[7] Dean Nelson, "India Election 2014: Narendra Modi Says India and Pakistan Should Be Allies in War on Poverty," The Telegraph, May 6, 2014.
[8] BJP Election Manifesto 2014.
[9] Andrew MacAskill, "Modi Eases Defense Investment Rules as India to Rebuild Forces," Bloomberg, July 10, 2014.
[10] Dilasha Seth, "DIPP proposes 100% FDI in Defence Sector," The Economic Times, May 30, 2014.
[11] Walter Ladwig, "India Sets Sail for Leadership," The Wall Street Journal, June 9, 2010.
[12] "Indian Navy: 11 Accidents, 22 Deaths in Seven Months," DnaIndia.com, March 7, 2014.
[13] T. P. Sreenivasan, "More Continuity, Less Change," The Indian Express, May 11, 2014.
[14] Lisa Curtis, "Enhancing India's Role in the Global Nonproliferation Regime," CSIS South Asia Program and the Nuclear Threat Initiative, December 2010.

Senator KAINE. Thank you very much. Great testimony all around, both the written testimony, which I found very provocative, and the presentations.

Two opportunities that I think are available to us that I just want to mark here. Mr. Singh, you mentioned the idea of a joint address to Congress. I am a cosponsor of a resolution we are currently working in the Senate that talks about sort of the new relationship with the United States and India, but it also includes a resolution to invite the Prime Minister to address Congress. I think that would send a very positive signal.

I also encourage and urge the administration to send a very positive signal in its choice of naming an ambassador to India. That is one of the strongest signals you can send. If you send someone—the kind of person you send, the identity of the person you send, the relationships that person already has in a country, and especially in a country whose partnership means so much to us, that is a very quick way to tell somebody how important they are. I really urge the administration to do that.

We are wrestling with our own significant challenges here in the Senate, frankly, about confirming ambassadors. It has been really discouraging to me that so many nations in the world with which we have so much business on the table right now have had vacancies in their ambassadorial posts, largely due to process issues here in the Senate that we ought to be able to resolve.

But to some degree, these matters also all begin with the administration naming a person. I think this particular vacancy gives the administration an opportunity to name someone that right away communicates a level of seriousness about the future of the relationship, and I encourage the administration to do it.

A couple of you have touched on an issue that I think is interesting, which is if we are looking at a way to strengthen this relationship going forward, there are positive things we can work on, but the other way to look at it is, what are the negative concerns that we ought to kind of sweep out of the way? We have concerns on our side—intellectual property, et cetera. But you are all experts at this and you all know the way the Indian leadership class kind of looks at these issues. What are concerns that they have right now with this government and the kind of new reality about the United States, about the relationship with the United States, that we ought to be thinking about about moving aside in these meetings that are coming up in the September visit of the Prime Minister here?

So educate me on, from the Indian perspective, what are concerns and issues that we ought to try to address and move aside so that they are not obstacles to a very productive future path? In whatever order you want. You do not have to go in the order.

Ambassador *Wisner.* I would be happy to throw the first stone, Senator.

Senator KAINE. Please.

Ambassador WISNER. In my testimony I made a point that I know is rooted in Indian perception. Indians are looking for a definition of how we intend to manage our affairs in protecting our security and the balance of power in Asia. They do not know what that is and it makes them profoundly uneasy because they do not know where they fit in, how we are going to manage Chinese power, how we are going to deal with Afghanistan, what are our plans toward Pakistan?

If I pick, at the top of my list of risks it is the risk of talking past each other. We select lots of specific initiatives that we can launch, but Indians are looking for a framework, an intellectual framework that will give them the ability to predict how America will react in a very tough time in history. That is what I hope the President and Kerry, the Secretary, and Secretary Hagel will really focus on: Get that right and so much will follow; risk number one.

Risk number two is known to all of us who have dealt with India over the years, and that is exaggerated expectations. India is not your normal ally; which accepts American solutions and from which we expect a degree of responsiveness to our ideas. India is a very reluctant partner, a very careful partner, a very suspicious partner.

The way you make the relationship work is not by setting your goals and expecting India to meet them, but a very careful discovery of what Indian goals and yours are and coming up with a meld. It is a different kind of diplomacy than the United States has been used to exercising. But I would argue the failure to do that puts a risk in the relationship, because once again we will talk past each other.

Mr. ROSSOW. I will just rattle off a couple of thoughts on this real quick. I think getting an ambassador to post, but at the same time I think what India would really like to see is somebody at the Cabinet level in the United States that they feel wakes up every day and thinks about India as one of the first few things. I think Ash Carter played that role. India felt that there was somebody in those high-level discussions that would think about India and their interests. But right now I do not know that they could point to somebody and say that that is our person.

I also think that for India's commercial interests the immigration bill, which the Senate passed and the House may take up at some point in the future, and its implications for IT service firms, also they continue to raise. I know this issue has never been quite elevated to that level of the totalization agreement on social security payments.

The last thing I will mention real quick, too, is there are two things happening this fall that will have a very pointed effect in the relationship. The USTR's out of cycle 301 review. Is India going to amend its patents law in a way that accommodates everybody's interests? I do not think that is likely to happen. So the 301 is going to be out there. It is going to be another roadblock we know is coming.

And the International Trade Commission has a report on India's trade barriers and I think even those of us that love the relationship realize there is a lot of barriers in India. The report is going to say that. So we have got two things coming up, two that we know are going to be poking at the relationship a little bit, mostly driven by things that the last government did. So reactions to that at the next government may be taken as unfair.

Senator KAINE. Mr. Rossow, just to follow up before the other witnesses answer the question, your point about the failed expectations syndrome; I guess there would be a danger if we as the United States deal with the new government kind of out of the basis of our experience with the previous government. That will be noticed and will not be appreciated. Your point was we kind of have to recognize that we have a big opportunity and if they set aside some precedent and do not feel bound by it then we should also approach it in a new way and not just based on past expectations.

Mr. ROSSOW. There is a very specific thing underlying that, which is that we dealt with them the Manmohan Singh government before, which was not the government of India. Sonya Gandhi, president of the party—and when we talk about the fact that the government could not get things done, if you were to look at Sonya Gandhi's legislative priorities she had almost a perfect batting record, including at the last minute, just months ago, passing a bill through Parliament amending the constitution to create a new state to try to save a few seats in their election. A very incredible legislative record, but that was not who we were dealing with, and that agenda was different than ours.

So the fact that we are dealing with the person in which power is consolidated in Delhi is a huge difference.

Senator KAINE. Thank you very much.

Mr. Singh.

Mr. SINGH. I echo a lot of what my colleagues have said, but I think the concerns of every Indian Government have been somewhat similar over the years. That is that if you get too close to the United States what does the United States get you stuck in? Where do you find yourself in an uncomfortable position? Where do you find yourself with deep ties, say on defense, that prove unreliable at a controversial time?

The mistrust that we have had over the years I think has almost entirely been eradicated. In fact, before the Khobragade incident I think that the sense was that we had basically overcome all of that kind of mistrust. But because relations are complicated between nations and because things like that incident happened or Snowden revelations happened to friends like Germany, really any relationship is subject to these kinds of bumps in the road.

But I think the Indians are particularly nervous about what being too close to the United States would actually mean. The shadow of nonalignment is not just a partisan thing. It is not just a Congress Party thing. It is there. It is a more positive vision when it comes from the current government, because it is not what we are not going to do; it is that we are going to be a nationalist government. And positive nationalism from this government could be a very powerful, useful thing, because it could give them a level of confidence to do things with us that have otherwise been thought of as somehow risky or suspect or things you would worry about.

But I actually think that there is a bigger—their concerns are not necessarily the main threats to us having a productive relationship. I think a lot of those concerns are fairly misplaced, especially now that you have such strong support for India across the board. Just look at the dynamism not only of your subcommittee, but look at the India Caucus on the Hill. It is very robust. So you have sort of really broad bipartisan support for the relationship.

But I think the thing that is a little more worrying, and it should be a concern to us and to them, is we are in a very complicated— it is a very complicated relationship and it is one where if it lacks leadership—that is to say, if the President and the Prime Minister are not fairly regularly making it clear to the two bureaucracies and the systems that their expectations are high and that problems should be resolved and that we should get through issues—we will not. The issues will eat us up in this relationship. The things that pop up, the obstacles, will—in anything we try to do, legal, policy, and other obstacles will pop up.

Those can either become insurmountable if they are sort of left in a vacuum of leadership or they can probably be relatively easily surmounted if there is regular leadership from above. So it is not enough for the two leaders to meet now and say we love each other, we want to have a good relationship. There has to be some real consistent mechanism. The infrastructure is there with the strategic dialogue, the high-level dialogues on defense. There are all these pieces. But somehow if it does not have that top-level leadership consistently applied, I do not think——

Senator KAINE. The bureaucracies are not capable of managing the relationship.

Mr. ROSSOW. Yes. They are very capable of bogging it down.

Senator KAINE. Yes, right, right. Thank you.

Ms. Curtis.

Ms. CURTIS. I think one of the biggest concerns I hear coming from Indians is the future of Afghanistan and our withdrawal. They are afraid we are going to withdraw too quickly and that we are going to allow Pakistan to drive the future of the country. I think there is major concern on this. So anything we can do to allay those concerns would be useful.

The second issue would be echoing what Rick mentioned in terms of the immigration issue and U.S. restrictions on the H1B visas and restriction on the numbers of highly skilled Indian workers coming into the United States. I think those would be the major issues.

Senator KAINE. Let me ask one other question and then I will see if Senator Risch has a question. I guess it was, Ambassador Wisner, your testimony was about this very ambitious economic goal of the 15 million jobs a year. Or, Mr. Rossow, was that your testimony? I cannot remember. So that is a huge and ambitious goal. So, going back to Ambassador Wisner's answer to my previous question, if the idea needs to be not just here is what we want, but let us really listen to what it is that this new government of India says it wants and then try to meld all of our goals together, if they are placing a very high priority on economic development, and in a pretty specific way—they have got a metric that is out there, a need to create 15 million jobs a year to deal with the changes in the population, the move of a rural population to the cities—that could be a focus of ours.

If we know that is their most significant goal, then there is a whole series of things—a manufacturing initiative, Mr. Rossow, you talked about—that we could do that I think would be mutually beneficial both for our interests and for theirs. But I am just kind of curious. Do all really see that significant economic acceleration as the primary goal right now that the Modi government wants to pursue and should we organize much of our thinking? We are not going to set side the good defense work we are doing, et cetera. Should we organize much of our thinking about how to work together around that very aggressive economic development goal?

Ambassador WISNER. Well, I think it is certainly one of the key objectives we have to reach for. I do not want to ignore other requirements. We have got real security interests in the continent. We want to work with India on those. We have issues that have to be addressed in terms of the broad economic picture, not just India and not just job creation.

But it really is vital, and it is going to be very tough. It is certainly a terrific focal point around which we can talk to Modi. Now, what really lies ahead? Fifteen million jobs, that is daunting. But at least we know that Modi is about growth. He is not about distribution first; he is about growth. So what kind of growth policies are going to work? He is looking for those. He is articulating them, and he has shown that once he finds them he uses the power of the office of the chief executive and he puts that strength behind it. He deals directly with his administration. His ministers really brand Modi's product the Civil Service Implements. Modi's India is more an executive model, less the classic Westminister model of Collective Cabinet Responsibility.

But to get there, Senator, I am going to repeat myself in one regard. I do not think simply investments in infrastructure, education, health are going to get 15 million jobs in India. We are all going through a complex time in the world in which job generation is very difficult to achieve. Now, how is India going to do it? Here again, if it models itself on the rest of the world as an open, competitive economy, where it invites the best of examples on how to grow and it does not hide behind barriers and tries to preserve a protective trade regime, then it has a chance of making that 15 million.

But if it does not do that, it is going to be a struggle. I think one of our top priorities ought to be, helping India think about how to open herself so she is competitive, taking the best examples around the world, adopting them herself, and then forcing them through.

Senator KAINE. Other thoughts about how the United States can help India achieve this goal? Mr. Singh?

Mr. SINGH. We often talk about what our businesses need, what we need to be able to do these sorts of things. I think Indian leaders have had historically a failure of explanation to their own people about why they need reforms to do things that Indian businesses need, that Indian workers need, that will actually help bring jobs.

That is not something we can articulate for them, but I do think that we should be poised to encourage the new government to do something that I think has really never been done before. Reforms were made, but they were almost made like: Do not look here; we are still going to do more of the social security safety net, we are still going to do more handouts, we are still going to maintain subsidies, we are still going to do all these other things; but, oh, we have got the opportunity to do some reforms.

What you have seen over the last 20 years is a plowing back. A lot of the economic benefit that came from the reforms started in the early nineties got plowed back into nonproductive activity. So they did not build themselves a virtuous cycle and they hoped for growth. They hoped for endless growth, and when growth stopped or stagnated they were caught even more unaware than some other countries in 2010. I think that was really a pretty rude awakening.

So the challenge is for a country that is used to a huge public sector in defense it is particularly daunting. Defense public sector undertakings in India are massive and inefficient and not very well suited to the kind of future that they are talking about wanting. And it is not just this government; the previous government, too. But they have not been able to politically see their way through that.

They have got to tell a good story. Modi has got to take the narrative "I will deliver good governance" and turn it into "And this is what that takes." He has said a lot of "This is why we have to do hard things," but what are those hard things and how do they deliver for the Indian people? And then he will have to show results.

The jobs thing is one indicator. He has also said he wants electricity to every Indian home in about a decade. There are 300 million Indian homes without electricity, so that is the equivalent of trying to produce electricity to the entire United States of America. That is daunting, and it can only be done if, as Ambassador Wisner says, they make real reforms.

Senator KAINE. Senator Risch had a back and forth with Ms. Biswal on the first panel about intellectual property and I thought she made an interesting point, and that was: We have very significant concerns about the intellectual property argument, but one of the ways that we would achieve what we would want is if the Indian private sector also came to realize, wow, better intellectual property protection is really going to help us as well. She seemed to indicate that there was a growing desire for more intellectual property protections within that domestic technology leadership in particular.

Do you share that? Do you see more of an embrace of intellectual property protection as driving policy with this new government?

Mr. ROSSOW. There is a couple of areas where industry has driven. We say "IP," but you are talking about patents.

Senator KAINE. Yes.

Mr. ROSSOW. That is what has driven this discussion. But if you look broadly at IP, pharma is an area where India lives based on generics production. It has never been leading edge in creating new molecules. But in other sectors that focus on IP—movies, TV, things like that, software, where India has been a leader—industry has done a lot of work to make sure that their government—that their interests are protected.

So I think it is going to be tougher in patents. We say "IP." I think in other areas of IP beyond patents there is a lot that has been done. For instance, on cable TV. There was rampant theft and illegal distribution of the channels that American companies and others created. They focused on digitization of cable TV, something that is being rolled out across the nation now, and 140 million homes have cable TV. This is a really big deal. And focusing on set-top boxes, making sure you knew who got what channels, that kind of stuff.

On films, it used to be that printed copies of films would be available on markets. So what India has done, industry-led, is digitization. So press of a button, they can transmit the films directly to the studios. So there is lots of work that the private sector has done and I think that kind of shows the case.

But in pharmaceuticals the problem is they are not there yet. They are not thinking this is going to be in their interest yet. So they are much further behind. But there is work—the domestic sector did get the message. They have shown to be quite leading edge.

Ambassador WISNER. Senator, to add a quick thought on what Rick said to you, to make it even sharper, we tend to say "intellectual property rights" and he is quite right, you have got to focus on those areas. One of the hottest topics for our pharmaceutical industry and what causes the most complaints is mandatory licensing. In fact the Indians have been involved in it only on rare occasions, but where they have done it they have frightened badly the international pharmaceutical industry. It believes steps taken in India will have international repercussions.

So when the USIBC chairman saw Modi on our recent trip he said: Prime Minister, the really key point is to have transparency and predictability, not to surprise people. He actually suggested, and Modi liked the idea, of putting together an Indian, international, and Indian Government panel to look at pharmaceutical issues and review them before the government makes its choices. Government is sovereign; what industry wants is a fair hearing.

So I think it is not going to be one law that can be written that is going to correct this, but a habit of consultation that will make a difference.

Senator KAINE. Senator Risch, questions.

Senator RISCH. Thank you. I am going to yield back, Mr. Chairman. My questions were answered. So thank you very much.

Senator KAINE. Thank you.

Let me ask a question about Iran. This is partly directly related to the India-Iran relationship, which there is a cultural tie that it has had that relationship over time. We give Iran a waiver to our sanctions regime—we give India a waiver to the sanctions regime for use of Iranian energy, largely out of a recognition partly of that cultural tie, but also partly because of the tremendous Indian need for energy.

What are the opportunities we might have to work with India—the civil nuclear power issue has been raised, or other areas—to help them develop their own native energy economy that might ultimately lead them to reduce their reliance upon Iranian energy? What opportunities are there?

Mr. ROSSOW. Well, I think India's got tough decisions to make for herself first, which is deregulating price controls of petroleum products. Most foreign companies will not go in and develop the resources. And the resources may be there. We have seen some large-ish natural gas and petroleum strikes over other rounds of licensing for private blocks for exploration and development. But foreign companies mostly have stayed away from doing that because you just do not know, with such a heavily regulated sector, as to whether or not whatever you find you are going to be able to market effectively at a price that makes it right.

So they have made steps. Even the Congress government made steps on loosening some price controls and reducing subsidies in this area. A lot more needs to be done, though. Until it is a fully transparent market where the government is not putting their finger on the scale every day, I think a lot of companies are going to stay away from really taking the dive and doing that in a bigger way.

Senator KAINE. But we would have an argument to make in consultation that the relaxation of that sort of overregulation or price control could achieve the 15 million year a goal of job growth. We could show our own track record of developing a really strong domestic energy economy and its connection to jobs if we are trying to help India reach that goal.

Mr. Singh.

Mr. SINGH. We mentioned the R&D and the work we are doing through the energy partnership on solar, which of course got subjected to local content requirements, which resulted in it being a trade dispute, basically. But trade disputes can bleed over into the energy cooperation.

There are huge potentials for cooperation in the energy sector, both in R&D, but also the Department of Energy could help India with technology for its own potential exploration, for the gas reserves that might be there that Rick was talking about.

It is interesting to note that I think one of the great signs of progress in our relationship was that India did make a concerted effort to reduce its purchasing from Iran when we were asking that that be something—when we were making it clear that that was something that was very important to the United States. And they did it in a way that I think really showed the maturing of the relationship as a strategic partnership. It does not prove that we are where we could be, but it was interesting to see how they handled that.

They really did try. They really were transparent. It was sort of, here is what we think we can achieve, and then we were able to come back and the administration was able to work closely with Congress to say, okay, we have got to figure out a way to square the circle here.

But they need energy growth and they need diversification and they need greater independence. So I think there is a lot of potential.

Senator KAINE. Lisa.

Ms. CURTIS. What immediately comes to mind is access to U.S. LNG exports. I think including them in that circle is something that is of interest.

But just to mention, with the relationship with Iran it is not just cultural, it is not just economics. They have strategic interest in the relationship with Iran because of their rivalry with Pakistan, but also because of the situation in Afghanistan, and their desire to prevent the Taliban from taking over there. They cooperated in the nineties against the Taliban in Afghanistan. So I just want to note that India also has strategic reasons for wanting to engage with Iran.

Senator KAINE. One last question that I have, and I raised this briefly with the first panel: Counterterrorism cooperation, the Mumbai attack, the presence of LET and the continued concerns about what their designs might be. What is the current status of the relationship between the United States and India in the counterterrorism area and what are some opportunities that we would have, that I think would be appreciated if we approached them with seriousness to help them really deal with that challenge? Because, as Ms. Curtis indicated in her testimony, any kind of an attack in the future, given the campaign sort of promises of P.M. Modi, he might have to respond in a particular way. So the best thing we could do is do everything we could to avoid that happening, and that involves CT cooperation.

What is the current status of the relationship?

Mr. SINGH. I will speak to it briefly. Post-Mumbai, we really transformed both law enforcement and intelligence cooperation. It has been really one of the more successful areas. The homeland security dialogue within the framework of the strategic dialogue is very productive. The intelligence relationship has been much more productive than people would have expected prior to 2008. We really do share a lot. We share threat information, but we also are sharing a lot of best practices for counterterrorism and other engagement. FBI, DHS, it is broad engagement, and it is good.

I think one area is cyber and intelligence-sharing, cyber in particular. I think the need for us to figure out a way to work more closely on cyber security could not be greater, and it has counterterrorism implications. We have a cyber security sort of information-sharing regime which sort of got going in 2010 or 2011, I think. It is the kind of thing that it needs to be updated almost constantly. Our engagement on cyber is really not something that you can just sort of do once and then say, okay, we are done. You have got to keep revisiting it. I think that would be an area to look to do more together.

So homeland defense, cyber, and intel-sharing are all areas in which we could have very productive additional engagement over what we are doing now.

Senator KAINE. Ms. Curtis.

Ms. CURTIS. I think we need to increase our engagement on regional terrorist threats. In talking about the Lashkar-e-Taiba, which is, of course, a threat to India, it also is important to remember the group is a threat to the United States—to the international community. The United States putting out a $10 million reward for information leading to the arrest or conviction of the leader of the LET, Hafiz Muhammad Saeed, was helpful because it showed that we are on the same page as India in terms of cracking down and trying to shut down these terrorist groups that are in the region.

Senator KAINE. Any additional thoughts on that, on that question? [No response.]

Well, let me just say this. This has been fantastic testimony. The written testimony was superb, provocative thoughts. We could stay here for hours and hours, but I want to take advantage of folks time. I really appreciate you all being here and helping us work through it.

It is an exciting moment in the relationship and I think we need not let the burdens of past expectations, failed expectations syndrome, wear us down. I think we can approach it as a fresh moment and think, not incrementally, but with a bigger vision about where we can go. You have made that very, very plain. We appreciate your being here today and look forward to more work together.

If there are members of the panel who do have questions to submit in writing, I will have them do that by 5 o'clock on Friday and would appreciate your solicitude in answering them should those questions occur.

With that, the hearing is adjourned.

[Whereupon, at 4:59 p.m., the hearing was adjourned.]

ADDITIONAL MATERIAL SUBMITTED FOR THE RECORD

RESPONSE OF NISHA BISWAL TO QUESTION
SUBMITTED BY SENATOR ROBERT MENENDEZ

Question. Ambassador Wisner suggested in his testimony that in an effort to promote transparency, Prime Minister Modi may be open to the establishment of a panel made up of the Indian Government as well as international and domestic private sector representatives that would review pharmaceutical issues before the Indian Government took decisions that impacted the industry.

- ♦ Has the U.S. raised the possibility of the establishment of this panel?
- ♦ Please describe the nature of U.S. engagement with the new Indian Government on intellectual property issues, particularly in the pharmaceutical field.

Answer. Protection of intellectual property rights (IPR) is a priority issue in the U.S.-India economic relationship. In our high-level engagements with India, notably in the Strategic Dialogue, Trade Policy Forum, and U.S.-India CEO Forum, we stress the benefits of creating an investor friendly environment, including by addressing IPR issues.

Transparency in the Government of India's decisionmaking process is one of the key issues detailed in the 2014 Special 301 Report. The United States would welcome any effort by the Government of India to make its system for protection and enforcement of IPR more predictable, transparent, and inclusive, including through the use of mechanisms such as panels, that would allow industries and service sectors, including the pharmaceutical sector, that rely on IPR to contribute to the policy- and decision-making process.

The U.S. interagency is planning to conduct an out-of-cycle review of U.S.-India engagement on IPR later this year and we will continue to work closely with our stakeholders across the IPR spectrum to identify ways to enhance IPR protection in India. These efforts will set the agenda for our work with the new Indian Government on IPR issues, especially as they affect the pharmaceutical sector.

RESPONSE OF NISHA BISWAL TO QUESTION SUBMITTED BY SENATOR MARCO RUBIO

Question. I am deeply disturbed by the 2-month investigative detention of U.S. citizen and Amway India CEO, Bill Pinckney, on what are basically civil issues. He has been imprisoned since May 26 on charges related to Prize Chits and Money Circulation Scheme (Banning) Act–1978.

- Can you give me an update on his status and describe what the Department of State is doing to secure his release?
- In your recent visits to India, have you brought up Mr. Pinckney's case with your Indian Government counterparts?

Answer. I am happy to report that Amway India CEO William S. Pinckney was released on bail on July 26. The U.S. Embassy in New Delhi and the U.S. Consulate General in Hyderabad remain in close touch with Mr. Pinckney, Amway, and the Indian authorities, and Mr. Pinckney is being provided with all appropriate U.S. consular services.

Mr. Pinckney's 2-month detention greatly concerned me and other U.S. Department of State officials, and we raised our concerns with the highest levels of the Indian Government. We welcome his release and will continue to monitor the situation closely.

www.ingramcontent.com/pod-product-compliance
Lightning Source LLC
Chambersburg PA
CBHW052012280526

45793CB00005B/952